Regulation of Information Technology in the European Union

Regulation of Information Technology in the European Union

Terry R. Broderick

KLUWER LAW INTERNATIONAL
LONDON / THE HAGUE / BOSTON

Published by:
Kluwer Law International
P.O. Box 85889, 2508 CN The Hague, The Netherlands
sales@kli.wkap.nl
http://www.kluwerlaw.com

Sold and Distributed in North, Central and South America by:
Kluwer Law International
657 Massachusetts Avenue, Cambridge, MA 02139, USA

Sold and Distributed in all other countries by:
Kluwer Law International
Distribution Centre, P.O. Box 322, 3300 AH Dordrecht, The Netherlands

Library of Congress Cataloging-in-Publication Data is available.

Printed on acid-free paper

ISBN 90-411-9823-7

Kluwer Law International incorporates the publishing programmes
of Graham & Trotman Ltd, Kluwer Law and Taxation Publishers
and Martinus Nijhoff Publishers

Printed and bound in Great Britain by Antony Rowe Limited.

CONTENTS

CHAPTER 1

INTRODUCTION

This book is an outgrowth of my specialized practice over nearly two decades in the field of European Union law. During that period, the focus has been on commercial transactions for information technology in the areas of international trade, competition policy, intellectual property, and regulatory developments.

Information technology is continuing to transform global communications and the world economy with innovative products and services. The markets exhibit a number of distinct characteristics:

- Fast-paced technological change including convergence with the audiovisual and telecommunications sectors.
- Substantial expenses for research and development with corresponding incentives to share costs by forming alliances and joint ventures.
- Products with decreasing life-cycles coupled with rapidly falling unit prices for commodity items such as personal computers and integrated circuits.
- Ongoing tension between open systems and proprietary standards.
- Transnational scope beyond the reach of any single regulatory body.

In this dynamic environment, events tend to be market-driven and it may be difficult for the regulators to keep up. The challenge for public authorities is to promote effective competition within a clear, coherent, and predictable framework: avoiding undue restrictions which might impede progress, cooperating with the private sector including appropriate reliance on industry self-regulation, and encouraging consistency on a multilateral basis to reflect the global nature of these activities.

The purpose of the book is to summarize the major rules and policies for information technology at European level. In doing so, I have attempted to provide essential background but without writing an exhaustive treatise on each subject. The result is a comprehensive overview as well as a good starting point for additional research on particular issues. As such, the book should be useful to anyone who is interested in a well-organized, straightforward explanation of the relevant principles. However, it is primarily intended as a handy reference for working professionals: practicing lawyers, corporate counsel, business executives, consultants, academics, and government or trade association officials.

A word about structure and organization: the book is in three basic parts. Chapters 2 and 3 describe the institutional framework and general policies for the "information society". Chapters 4 through 6 cover the detailed rules for external trade, competition, and intellectual property. Finally, Chapter 7 discusses the Internet and electronic commerce. The sources cited are current as of May 26, 2000.

I have tried to be conscientious and thorough in preparing this material. Any errors are solely my responsibility. For answers to specific legal questions, including implementation of European measures at the national level, the traditional advice remains the best: you should consult with competent counsel.

CHAPTER 2

INSTITUTIONAL FRAMEWORK

This overview of the institutional framework in the European Union identifies the principal players and briefly describes how the system operates. The sections below cover the historical background, Member States, major agencies, legislative process, and efforts to create a single European market through the elimination of technical barriers. Throughout, there are references to appropriate Internet addresses which provide additional information on particular subjects.

1. BACKGROUND

The European Economic Community (EEC) was established by the Treaty of Rome in 1957. Since then, this has been the primary legal basis for the regulation of private commercial activity including information technology at European level. The major amendments to the original Treaty are summarized below:

- *Single European Act (1987)*: reforms to improve the decision-making process particularly in connection with the program for completion of the internal Community market by December 1992. For details, see Section 5 on the elimination of technical barriers.
- *Maastricht Treaty (1992)*: replacement of "EEC" with "European Community" (EC), adoption of the term "European Union" (EU) to describe the broader movement toward political integration, and enactment of the provisions for introduction of a common European currency from January 1999.[1]
- *Amsterdam Treaty (1997)*: further developments including the extension of qualified-majority voting in the Council of Ministers and increased use of the co-decision procedure for legislation involving the European Parliament. This became effective in May 1999.[2]

[1] The centerpiece of the program for a common currency was the adoption of the "Euro" (EUR) by all the Member States except Denmark, Greece, Sweden, and the U.K. This replaced the former European Currency Unit (ECU) at a ratio of one-to-one and will be substituted throughout the remaining text for purposes of clarity. Introduction of the Euro was accompanied by a new exchange-rate mechanism (ERM II) which links it to the currencies of the non-participating Member States.

[2] This incorporates a consolidated version of the revised EC Treaty which includes the renumbering of key articles. The current provisions will be cited throughout but with explanatory references to the former articles as appropriate.

2. Member States

As a result of the latest round of enlargement in January 1995, the EU now comprises the following 15 Member States:[3]

– Austria	– Germany	– Netherlands
– Belgium	– Greece	– Portugal
– Denmark	– Ireland	– Spain
– Finland	– Italy	– Sweden
– France	– Luxembourg	– United Kingdom

3. Major Agencies

These include the European Parliament, Council of Ministers, Commission, Court of Justice, and other selected entities. Basic information on all the EU institutions, along with direct access to their home pages, can be located on the Europa Internet server at *www.europa.eu.int.*

3.1. European Parliament[4]

The Parliament is based in Strasbourg and consists of 626 members elected to five-year terms. Historically, their role was essentially consultative, but they now participate more directly in legislation with the Council of Ministers under the co-decision and cooperation procedures. Activities concerning information technology are covered by the committees listed below:

- Legal Affairs and Internal Market,
- Industry, External Trade, Research, and Energy,
- Employment and Social Affairs,
- Culture, Youth, Education, the Media, and Sport.

3.2. Council of Ministers[5]

The Council has one representative from each Member State and is primarily responsible for the final enactment of Community legislation except when operating jointly with the Parliament. Meetings are held in Brussels and Luxembourg under a presidency which rotates every six months in accordance with a prescribed schedule. Depending on the circumstances, the Council makes decisions by unanimity, simple majority, or qualified majority. They are assisted by a Committee of Permanent Representatives (COREPER) which prepares their work and performs designated tasks.

---

3 Article 299 of the EC Treaty (former Article 227).

4 Articles 189–201 of the EC Treaty (former Articles 137–144).

5 Articles 202–210 of the EC Treaty (former Articles 145–154).

3.3. European Commission[6]

The Commission is headquartered in Brussels and is the EU's major executive agency with 20 members appointed to five-year terms. They are charged with initiating and implementing Community legislation, and exercise quasi-judicial powers in enforcing provisions such as the competition rules of the Treaty.

The Commission website is at *europa.eu.int/comm*. For administrative purposes, they are divided internally into numerous specialized Directorates-General. A full listing can be found at *europa.eu.int/comm/dgs*. These share certain overlapping functions for information technology, but the unit with the most comprehensive responsibility is the Directorate-General for the Information Society (*europa.eu.int/comm/dgs/information_society*) which is further sub-divided as follows:

- Communication services policy and regulatory framework,
- Systems and services for the citizen,
- New methods of work and electronic commerce,
- Content, multimedia tools and market,
- Essential technologies and infrastructure,
- Generic technological developments and horizontal actions.

In addition, as part of the "e-Europe" initiative, the Information Society Directorate-General has established a special site to consolidate developments relating to digital technologies and electronic commerce (*europa.eu.int/comm/information_society/eeurope*). This is referenced further at Section 1 of Chapter 3 and Section 5.1 of Chapter 7 below.

Other support is provided by an Information Society Activities Center, Information Society Promotion Office, and European Internet Forum, all located in Brussels, which coordinate efforts, make recommendations, and furnish material to the public. See also the detailed information at *www.ispo.cec.be*.

3.4. European Court of Justice[7]

The Court of Justice is the final arbiter for the interpretation of Community law. It is assisted by the Court of First Instance as an intermediate tribunal in specified cases. Each is based in Luxembourg and has 15 judges appointed to six-year terms.

3.5. Others

Among the remaining Community agencies, it is worth mentioning the Economic and Social Committee and the Committee of the Regions.[8] Both are consultative bodies which occasionally issue advisory opinions on the subject of information technology.

---

[6] Articles 211–219 of the EC Treaty (former Articles 155–163).

[7] Articles 220–245 of the EC Treaty (former Articles 164–188).

[8] Articles 257–265 of the EC Treaty (former Articles 193–198c).

4. LEGISLATION[9]

This comprises a number of different elements as indicated below:

- *Regulations*: directly applicable and binding on the Member States without further legislation at the national level.
- *Directives*: binding on each Member State for the result to be achieved, but with the form and method left for national authorities to enact by a fixed date.
- *Decisions*: specific rulings binding on the Member States, companies, or individuals concerned.
- *Recommendations, opinions, and resolutions*: non-binding statements to encourage particular practices.

All the elements of legislation are published in the *Official Journal of the European Communities* (OJ) and appear in electronic form at the Eur-Lex website (*europa.eu.int/eur-lex*).

The Commission issues other selected items including communications, notices, and Green or White Papers. These are variously intended to provide interpretive guidance on Community policies, announce proposals for legislation, or serve as consultative documents to encourage discussion among interested parties on possible subjects for regulation.

5. ELIMINATION OF TECHNICAL BARRIERS

5.1. Mutual Recognition

As part of the effort to create a genuine internal market, the EU initially attempted to dismantle technical barriers to trade among Member States by developing detailed standards for individual products through specific legislation which would preempt national requirements and apply on a Community-wide basis. This proved time-consuming and ineffective, and was eventually superseded by their new approach based on the principle of "mutual recognition" in 1985.[10]

In accordance with this procedure, the EU issues harmonization directives prescribing the "essential requirements" necessary to ensure adequate protection for consumers, public health, and the environment. Compliance with those criteria is mandatory. Otherwise, Member States are free to enact their own legislation consistent with the general rules and must in turn recognize the validity of appropriate implementing measures taken by other Member States.

---

[9] Articles 249–256 of the EC Treaty (former Articles 189–192).

[10] See the Council resolution on a "new approach" to technical harmonization and standards, OJ No. C136/1 (June 4, 1985), as well as the communication from the Commission published at COM(85)17 final (January 31, 1985). The principle of "mutual recognition" was established by the Court of Justice in a line of decisions interpreting Article 28 et seq. of the Treaty (former Article 30 et seq.) beginning with *Rewe-Zentral v. Bundesmonopolverwaltung fuer Branntwein,* Case No. 120/78, 1979 European Court Reports (ECR) 649, 1979-3 Common Market Law Reports (CMLR) 494. For the latest statement in this area, see the Council resolution on mutual recognition at OJ No. C141/5 (May 19, 2000).

5.2. New Barriers

Preventing new barriers is an important corollary to the elimination of existing restrictions. For that reason, Directive No. 98/34 requires Member States to provide notice of draft technical standards and regulations before adoption.[11] This includes a standstill obligation for specified time periods to permit prior review, consultation, and the potential initiation of Community legislation on the relevant subject. The Commission considers national measures implemented in violation of these procedures to be invalid.[12]

An amendment to Directive No. 98/34 expressly extends these requirements to information society services.[13] This covers services normally provided for remuneration, at a distance, by electronic means and at the individual request of the recipient.[14] Under Article 1(2), it does not apply to radio broadcasting or to television broadcasting within the scope of Article 1(a) of Directive No. 89/552. In addition, Article 1(5) and Annex 6 make the Directive inapplicable to:

- Matters covered by other Community legislation for telecommunications services as defined by Directive No. 90/387 or financial services including banking, insurance, investment activities, and pension funds.
- Rules concerning regulated markets within the meaning of Directive No. 93/22 except for the requirement to communicate definitive texts under Article 8(3).

5.3. Standards and Specifications

Development of detailed product specifications to promote interoperability is outside the scope of the harmonization directives and is being encouraged by the Community through the work of standardization agencies.[15] The most important are:

- European Committee for Standardization (CEN),
- European Committee for Electrotechnical Standardization (CENELEC),
- European Telecommunications Standards Institute (ETSI).

Compliance with their specifications remains voluntary, but has the significant advantage of creating a presumption of conformity with the "essential requirements" at Section 5.1 above. The Commission is playing an active role in this area by supporting other interested

[11] Directive No. 98/34 of the European Parliament and Council laying down a procedure for the provision of information in the field of technical standards and regulations, OJ No. L204/37 (July 21, 1998). This consolidates and supersedes the requirements in Council Directive No. 83/189, OJ No. L109/8 (April 26, 1983), as amended.

[12] See the communication from the Commission at OJ No. C245/4 (October 1, 1986). This position was upheld by the Court of Justice in *CIA Security International v. Signalson*, Case No. C-194/94, 1996 ECR 1-2201, 1996-2 CMLR 781.

[13] Directive No. 98/48 of the European Parliament and Council amending Directive No. 98/34 laying down a procedure for the provision of information in the field of technical standards and regulations, OJ No. L217/18 (August 5, 1998). Article 2 of Directive No. 98/48 calls upon the Member States to enact appropriate implementing measures by August 5, 1999.

[14] See Article 1(2) and Annex 5 of Directive No. 98/34 as amended.

[15] See the Council resolution on the role of standardization in Europe, OJ No. C141/1 (May 19, 2000); communication from the Commission on standardization in the global information society, COM(96)359

parties in the development of standards and specifications for the information society.[16] The current state of play, including links to CEN, CENELEC, and ETSI, can be found at *www.newapproach.org*.

5.4. Testing and Certification

To supplement the harmonization directives, the Council has established various "modules" comprising a uniform system to evaluate the design and manufacture of products for compliance with the "essential requirements".[17] These include a manufacturer's declaration for internal production control, a full "EC-type examination" where a competent technical agency determines whether a product meets the relevant standards, and other detailed provisions for quality control. Individual directives permit a range of modules for each product in order to give manufacturers as much discretion as possible consistent with their obligations for health and safety. The directives contain criteria for choosing the most appropriate module from among the available options.

(July 24, 1996); Council resolution on the role of European standardization in the European economy, OJ No. C173/1 (July 9, 1992); Commission communication on the development of European standardization, OJ No. C20/1 (January 28, 1991); Council resolution on standardization in the field of information technology and telecommunications, OJ No. C117/1 (May 11, 1989); and Council Decision No. 87/95 on standardization in the field of information technology and telecommunications, OJ No. L36/31 (February 7, 1987).

16 For example, see the Commission call for proposals on standardization projects for the information society (ISIS), OJ No. C144/12 (May 22, 1999).

17 See Council Decisions No. 93/465 and No. 90/683 at OJ No. L220/23 (August 30, 1993) and OJ No. L380/13 (December 31, 1990), respectively.

CHAPTER 3

INFORMATION SOCIETY

The term "information society" is used for a diverse assortment of policies designed to help Europe benefit from advances in electronic communications. This chapter summarizes the key elements including items for the convergence of technology, research and development, trans-European networks, product liability, and the Y2K or millennium problem. Subjects which relate more specifically to the Internet and electronic commerce are covered at Chapter 7 below.

1. General

Early efforts in this area focused on measures to enhance the competitiveness of European industry in the application of specific technologies such as data-processing and microelectronics.[1] The first integrated Community "action plan" was established in 1988 with the aim of reducing legal and economic uncertainty, promoting the use of electronic information services, and encouraging cooperation between the public and private sectors on pilot and demonstration projects.[2] This was extended through 1995 with an expanded range of activities for improving the understanding of the internal information market, overcoming legal and technical barriers, increasing user-friendliness and information literacy, and supporting strategic initiatives.[3]

The current action plan is based on a series of studies undertaken by the Commission from 1994 to 1996.[4] This includes an amalgam of policies for the "information society"[5]

---

1 Council resolution on a Community action promoting microelectronics technology, OJ No. C231/1 (September 13, 1979), and Council resolution on a Community policy for data-processing, OJ No. C86/1 (July 20, 1974).

2 Council Decision No. 88/524 on establishment of a plan of action for setting up an information services market, OJ No. L288/39 (October 21, 1988).

3 Council Decision No. 91/691 adopting a program for establishment of an internal information services market, OJ No. L377/41 (December 31, 1991).

4 Commission communication on Europe and the global information society: a developing plan of action, COM(96)607 (November 27, 1996); Commission communication on the information society: from Corfu to Dublin, the new emerging priorities – implications of the information society for EU policies, COM(96)395 (July 24, 1996); and Commission communication on Europe's way to the information society: an action plan, COM(94)347 (July 19, 1994).

5 See generally the Commission communication on globalization and the information society: the need for strengthened international coordination, COM(98)50 (February 4, 1998); Commission communication on the competitiveness of European information technology industries, COM(97)152 (April 16, 1997); Council resolution on new policy priorities regarding the information society, OJ No. C376/1 (December 12, 1996);

incorporating a number of disparate elements:

– *Creation of a favorable business climate:*
  - Timely production of suitable standards and specifications.[6]
  - Research critical to the development of technology and applications in multimedia products and services.
  - Appropriate use of internal market principles and competition policy to encourage innovation and investment.
  - Effective protection and enforcement of intellectual property rights.
  - Improved financing mechanisms for the provision of risk capital.
  - Special incentives for small- and medium-sized firms.

– *Social, cultural and other aspects*:[7]
  - Education and training to meet changing work requirements and adaptation to new forms of employment.
  - Emphasis on cultural and linguistic diversity.
  - Consumer safeguards and related issues.
  - Protection of fundamental rights such as confidentiality of personal data and regulation of illegal content in material distributed over electronic networks.
  - Economic and social cohesion including the elimination of regional disadvantages by making the benefits of the information society widely available.
  - Environmental protection.

– *International dimension*:
  - Free and fair trade and competition.
  - Multilateral rules for non-discriminatory market access.
  - Agreed framework for cooperation in the use of global information networks.

Council resolution on industrial aspects for the EU in the development of the information society, OJ No. C341/5 (December 19, 1995); Bangemann report on Europe and the global information society, cited in the General Report on the Activities of the European Union (EU General Report) 1994 at ¶397; Commission White Paper on growth, competitiveness, and employment, COM(93)700 (December 5, 1993); Council resolution on electronics, information, and communications technologies, OJ No. C325/2 (December 14, 1991); and Commission communication on the European electronics and information technology industry: state of play, issues at stake, and proposals for action, cited in the EU General Report 1991 at ¶278 and ¶366.

6 See the references in Section 5.3 of Chapter 2 above.

7 See Council resolution on the employment and social dimension of the information society, OJ No. C8/1 (January 12, 2000); Commission Decision No. 1999/698 establishing ecological criteria for the award of the Community eco-label to portable computers, OJ No. L276/7 (October 27, 1999); Commission Decision No. 1999/205 establishing ecological criteria for the award of the Community eco-label to personal computers, OJ No. L70/46 (March 17, 1999); Decision No. 283/1999 of the European Parliament and Council establishing a general framework for Community activities in favor of consumers, OJ No. L34/1 (February 9, 1999); Council resolution on the consumer dimension of the information society, OJ No. C23/1 (January 28, 1999); Commission communication on the social and labor market dimension of the information society: people first – the next steps, COM(97)390 (July 23, 1997); Council Decision No. 96/664 on adoption of a multiannual program to promote the linguistic diversity of the Community in the information society, OJ No. L306/40 (November 28, 1996); and Commission Green Paper on living and working in the information society: people first, COM(96)389 (July 24, 1996).

- *Supporting measures in related areas*:
  - Audiovisual sector: development of the European multimedia content industry and new information services.[8]
  - Telecommunications liberalization: competitive markets for expansion and growth, interoperability, and interconnection including links between public databases in the Member States.[9]

More recently, the Council has adopted a multiannual program to stimulate the establishment of the information society in Europe which covers the period 1998–2002.[10] The objectives are to increase public awareness and understanding, optimize socio-economic

---

[8] See Commission communication on a proposal for a program in support of the audiovisual industry (Media Plus 2001–2005), COM(99)658 (December 14, 1999); Commission communication on principles and guidelines for the Community's audiovisual policy in the digital age, COM(99)657 (December 14, 1999); Council Decision No. 1999/297 establishing a Community statistical information infrastructure relating to the industry and markets of the audiovisual and related sectors, OJ No. L117/39 (May 5, 1999); Directive No. 97/36 of the European Parliament and Council amending Directive No. 89/552 on the coordination of provisions in the Member States concerning television broadcasting activities, OJ No. L202/60 (July 30, 1997); Council Decision No. 96/339 adopting a multiannual Community program to stimulate the development of a European multimedia content industry (INFO 2000), OJ No. L129/24 (May 30, 1996); and Council Decision No. 95/563 on the implementation of a program encouraging the development and distribution of European audiovisual works (Media II, 1996–2000), OJ No. L321/25 (December 30, 1995).

[9] See Commission communication: towards a new framework for electronic communications infrastructure and associated services – the 1999 communications review, COM(99)539 (November 10, 1999). A selection of the relevant legislation includes Commission Directive No. 1999/64 to ensure that telecommunications networks and cable networks owned by a single operator are separate legal entities, OJ No. L175/39 (July 10, 1999); Directive No. 1999/5 of the European Parliament and Council on radio equipment and telecommunications terminal equipment and the mutual recognition of their conformity, OJ No. L91/10 (April 7, 1999); Directive No. 98/10 of the European Parliament and Council on the application of open network provision to voice telephony and universal service for telecommunications in a competitive environment, OJ No. L101/24 (April 1, 1998); Directive No. 97/66 of the European Parliament and Council on the processing of personal data and the protection of privacy in the telecommunications sector, OJ No. L24/1 (January 30, 1998); Directive No. 97/33 of the European Parliament and Council on interconnection in telecommunications for universal service and interoperability through application of the principles of open network provision, OJ No. L199/32 (July 26, 1997); Directive No. 97/13 of the European Parliament and Council on a common framework for general authorizations and individual licenses in the field of telecommunications services, OJ No. L117/15 (May 7, 1997); Commission Directive No. 96/19 on implementation of full competition in telecommunications markets, OJ No. L74/13 (March 22, 1996); Commission Directive No. 96/2 on mobile and personal communications, OJ No. L20/59 (January 26, 1996); Directive No. 95/47 of the European Parliament and Council on the use of standards for the transmission of television signals, OJ No. L281/51 (November 23, 1995); Commission Directive No. 95/51 on abolition of restrictions on the use of cable television networks for the provision of already liberalized telecommunications services, OJ No. L256/49 (October 26, 1995); Council Directive No. 92/44 on the application of open network provision to leased lines, OJ No. L165/27 (June 19, 1992); Council Directive No. 91/263 on approximation of the laws of the Member States concerning telecommunications terminal equipment including mutual recognition of their conformity, OJ No. L128/1 (May 23, 1991); Commission Directive No. 90/388 on competition in the markets for telecommunications services, OJ No. L192/10 (July 24, 1990); and Council Directive No. 90/387 on establishment of the internal market for telecommunications services through implementation of open network provision, OJ No. L192/1 (July 24, 1990).

[10] OJ No. L107/10 (April 7, 1998).

benefits, and highlight Europe's global role. This is being augmented by a special "e-Europe" initiative to help modernize the Community economy through rapid introduction of digital technologies and the requisite underlying skills. For additional details, see Section 3.3 of Chapter 2 and Section 5.1 of Chapter 7.

2. Convergence of Technology

Information technology traditionally encompasses computer equipment, software, and services such as consulting, out-sourcing, and systems integration. However, dramatic advances in digitalization and the rapid growth of the Internet are beginning to blur the standard categories and lead to increasing convergence with telecommunications and the media in the transmission of data, text, sound, and pictures.

As indicated in the preceding section, Community policies for the information society already incorporate certain supporting elements for the audiovisual and telecommunications sectors. The Commission is now considering whether regulatory structures should be fundamentally adapted to reflect the reality and pace of convergence.[11] This is still at an early stage but initial consultations have identified a number of agreed principles as the basis for further analysis and reform:[12]

- Regulation should be clear, proportional, and transparent.
- It should promote public interest objectives as well as investment in new services.
- There should be common rules for the transmission of signals via networks and infrastructure coupled with a sector-specific approach to content.
- Effective application of competition policy is essential in the new multimedia environment.
- Steps should be taken to promote European content and the benefits of public broadcasting.

3. Research and Development

The Community's fourth framework program for research and development allocated EUR 3.405 billion to information and communications technologies from 1994 to 1998.[13]

---

11 Commission Green Paper on convergence of the telecommunications, media, and information technology sectors and the implications for regulation: towards an information society approach, COM(97)623 (December 3, 1997). See also the resolution of the European Parliament at OJ No. C341/136 (November 9, 1998), and the opinions by the Economic and Social Committee and the Committee of the Regions at OJ No. C214/79 (July 10, 1998) and OJ No. C373/26 (December 2, 1998), respectively.

12 Commission communication on the results of the public consultation on the Green Paper on convergence of the telecommunications, media, and information technology sectors and the implications for regulation, COM(99) 108 (March 9, 1999). See also the Council conclusions on the results of the public consultations on the Convergence Green Paper (in particular the aspects relating to the media and audiovisual sector), OJ No. C283/1 (October 6, 1999), and the opinion by the Committee of the Regions at OJ No. C57/5 (February 29, 2000).

13 Decision No. 1110/94 of the European Parliament and Council concerning the fourth framework program of the EC activities in the field of research and technological development and demonstration (1994–1998),

These activities were implemented by specific decisions in the fields of advanced communications, telematics, and information technology.[14] The detailed program for information technology emphasized user-requirements and market-driven policies for new infrastructure in each of the following areas:

- Software and distributed information processing.
- Components and sub-systems including microelectronics and peripherals.
- Multimedia systems.
- Long-term research.
- Focused clusters involving industrial applications for open microprocessor systems, high-performance computing and networking, technologies for business processes, and integration in manufacturing.

Additional efforts are now underway in accordance with the fifth framework program which runs through 2002.[15] This includes a major initiative for the "user-friendly information society," supported by planned funding of EUR 3.6 billion, to address issues such as access, ease of use, cost-effectiveness, interoperability, standardization, and socio-economic impact.[16] Implementation of the program is based on the "key actions" and related measures summarized below:[17]

- *Systems and services for the citizen*: the environment, health care, special needs of the elderly and disabled, public administrations, transport and tourism.
- *New methods of work and electronic commerce*: flexible and remote employment, management systems for suppliers and consumers, information and network security.
- *Multimedia content and tools*: interactive electronic publishing, education and training, language technologies, advanced methods for accessing and handling information.
- *Essential technologies and infrastructure*: information processing and networks, software and services, techniques for real-time and large-scale simulation and visualization, satellite-based mobile and personal communications, microelectronics, interfaces, peripherals, sub-systems.

OJ No. L126/1 (May 18, 1994). These expenditures were later increased by the measures at OJ No. L86/69 (April 4, 1996) and OJ No. L347/1 (December 18, 1997).

[14] See the Council Decisions at OJ No. L222/35 (August 26, 1994), OJ No. L334/1 (December 22, 1994), and OJ No. L334/24 (December 22, 1994), respectively. There was also a specific program for cooperation with third countries and international organizations, OJ No. L334/109 (December 22, 1994). A practical example is the joint project for research and development on intelligent manufacturing systems between the EU and Australia, Canada, Japan, Norway, Switzerland, and the U.S. See OJ No. L161 (June 18, 1997).

[15] Decision No. 182/1999 of the European Parliament and Council concerning the fifth framework program of the EC for research, technological development, and demonstration activities (1998–2002), OJ No. L26/1 (February 1, 1999).

[16] See Article 1(2) and Annexes II and III of Decision No. 182/1999.

[17] See Annex II of Decision No. 182/1999 as well as Council Decision No. 1999/168 adopting a specific program for research, technological development, and demonstration on a user-friendly information society (1998–2002), OJ No. L64/20 (March 12, 1999). See also Commission Decision No. 98/610 setting up expert groups to assist on the content and orientation of the key actions in the field of research and technological development, OJ No. L290/57 (October 29, 1998), and Commission Decision No. 98/611 on the creation of the European Research Forum, OJ No. L290/61 (October 29, 1998).

- *Generic activities*: nano-scale, quantum, photonic, and bio-electronic technologies including future generation integrated circuits, ultra-high-performance computers, and super intelligent networks.
- *Research infrastructures*: implementation and interoperability of Europe-wide advanced high-speed computer and communication systems for research in connection with the global evolution of the Internet.

4. Trans-European Networks

In addition to funding research, the Community actively promotes useful application of the results through a number of trans-European networks:

- *Electronic data interchange (EDI)*: this program extended from 1988 to 1994 and encouraged the development of pan-European EDI to improve industrial competitiveness.[18] It covered standardization of EDI messages, legal aspects, message security, multisector projects, information campaigns, and analysis of the impact on company management. The Commission also endorsed a European model agreement for EDI which provides a flexible and concrete approach to the legal issues involved in cooperation between parties for the exchange of electronic messages.[19]
- *Network infrastructure*: work in this area aims to ensure interconnection and interoperability for the harmonized introduction of the European integrated services digital network (Euro-ISDN). The goal is eventual movement to integrated broadband communication (IBC) networks, including asynchronous transfer mode (ATM), as the optimum platform for multimedia information society applications.[20]
- *Public administrations*: the focus here is on telematics for the electronic exchange of data between Community agencies and public authorities in the different Member States. Examples are the Edicom program for statistics on the trading of goods[21] and the IDA initiative for interchange of data between administrations on projects of common interest.[22] The Commission is also considering how the information gathered by

[18] See Council Decision No. 87/499 introducing a communications network Community program on trade electronic data interchange systems (TEDIS), OJ No. L285/35 (October 8, 1987), and Council Decision No. 91/385 establishing the second phase of the TEDIS program, OJ No. L208/66 (July 30, 1991).

[19] Commission recommendation on the legal aspects of electronic data interchange, OJ No. L338/98 (December 28, 1994). This is discussed in greater detail in Section 5.4 of Chapter 7 below.

[20] Decision No. 2717/95 of the European Parliament and Council on a set of guidelines for the development of Euro-ISDN, OJ No. L282/16 (November 24, 1995), and Decision No. 1336/97 of the European Parliament and Council on a series of guidelines for trans-European telecommunications networks, OJ No. L183/12 (July 11, 1997).

[21] Council Decision No. 96/715 on inter-administration telematic networks for statistics on the trading of goods between Member States (Edicom), OJ No. L327/34 (December 18, 1996).

[22] Council Decision No. 95/468 on a Community contribution for telematic interchange of data between administrations in the Community (IDA), OJ No. L269/23 (November 11, 1995). This was subsequently

public agencies might be disseminated more widely and effectively to benefit private individuals and businesses in Europe.[23]

5. Product Liability

The EU Product Liability Directive establishes a system of liability without fault for damage caused by defective products.[24] This applies to all movables including both finished goods and components.[25] Under Article 4 of the Directive, an injured party is required to prove damage, defect, and a causal relationship. A product is considered defective when it fails to provide the safety which a person is entitled to expect taking all the circumstances into account, but not for the sole reason that a better product is later put on the market.[26] Article 7 lists a number of affirmative defenses including:

- The state of scientific and technical knowledge at the time did not permit discovery of the defect.
- For defective components, that a problem is attributable to the design of the finished product or the instructions given by the manufacturer.[27]

Liability is joint and several and covers personal injury as well as property damage.[28] The statute of limitations is three years and rights are extinguished ten years after the product is first put into circulation.[29]

In addition to the foregoing Directive, other rules generally require that only safe products be placed on the market.[30] These include provisions for the rapid exchange of information among the Community and Member States in emergency situations which may

---

invalidated by the Court of Justice for an improper legal basis, but without prejudice to implementing measures already taken. See *European Parliament v. Council*, Case No. C-22/96, OJ No. C234/11 (July 25, 1998). The IDA program has been extended by Decisions No. 1719/1999 and No. 1720/1999 of the European Parliament and Council, OJ No. L203/1 and OJ No. L203/9 (August 3, 1999), respectively.

23 Commission Green Paper on public sector information in the information society, COM(98)585 (January 20, 1999). See also the opinions by the Economic and Social Committee and the Committee of the Regions at OJ No. C169/30 (June 16, 1999) and OJ No. C57/11 (February 29, 2000), respectively.

24 Council Directive No. 85/374 on the approximation of the laws, regulations, and administrative provisions of the Member States concerning liability for defective products, OJ No. L210/29 (August 7, 1985), as amended by Directive No. 1999/34 of the European Parliament and Council, OJ No. L141/20 (June 4, 1999).

25 Articles 2 and 3 of Directive No. 85/374.

26 Article 6 of Directive No. 85/374.

27 See also the Council resolution on operating instructions for technical consumer goods, OJ No. C411/1 (December 31, 1998), which indicates that inadequate instructions may be a factor in evaluating whether goods are defective.

28 Articles 5 and 9 of Directive No. 85/374. This is without prejudice to national laws on “non-material damage.” Article 13 also indicates that other rules of contractual or non-contractual liability may continue to apply.

29 Articles 10 and 11 of Directive No. 85/374.

30 Council Directive No. 92/59 on general product safety, OJ No. L228/24 (August 11, 1992). The Commission is proposing amendments to Directive No. 92/59 which would require more effective surveillance and rapid intervention for dangerous products including a prohibition on export to third countries. See Commission press-release IP(00)309 (March 29, 2000).

lead to the recall of items creating a serious and immediate risk to the health and safety of consumers.

At present, there is no comprehensive Community-wide legislation on the liability of suppliers of services.[31] Specific measures relating to the emerging area of electronic commerce are discussed in Chapter 7 below.

6. Millennium Problem

The millennium or year 2000 (Y2K) problem was a particular kind of dysfunction caused by the inability of certain software, which uses only two digits to indicate the year, to process information correctly for dates after December 31, 1999. This included embedded systems in microprocessors with pervasive applications in areas such as avionics and traffic management, and might have led to chain-reaction failures from individual breakdowns with knock-on effects on upstream or downstream operations. It was viewed as a significant source of potential liability for both personal injury and property damage within the meaning of the Product Liability Directive discussed in the preceding section. The vulnerable period was not limited to January 1, 2000 since systemic errors could occur both before and after that date.

For the Community, this situation was even more troublesome because of the major ongoing project to adapt data-processing requirements for the transition to a single European currency from January 1999. The Commission has noted that "taken together both problems represent a challenge of unprecedented scale for the information technology sector. …"[32] In their view, the basic responsibility rested with suppliers and users of computer-based systems, but with an important supporting role for European authorities.[33] Relevant precautions included:

- Ensuring the effectiveness of their own internal operating systems and establishing an inter-service task force, specific office, and Internet website (*www.ispo.cec.be/y2keuro*) as designated contact points for interested parties.
- Working closely with Member States to assess the readiness of their central and local administrations, interconnection with other countries, and contingency plans for the continuity of vital public services and infrastructure.[34]

---

[31] The Commission's earlier proposal on this subject was never finally enacted. See OJ No. C12/8 (January 18, 1991).

[32] Commission press-release IP(98)183 (February 25, 1998). For additional statements on the combined impact of the technological problems arising from the millennium and the single European currency, see the Commission responses to inquiries from the European Parliament at OJ No. C135/126 (May 14, 1999), OJ No. C323/37 (October 21, 1998), OJ No. C310/61-62 (October 9, 1998), OJ No. C304/31 (October 2, 1998), OJ No. C304/98 (October 2, 1998), and OJ No. C196/42 (June 22, 1998).

[33] See the Commission communication on the Year 2000 computer problem, COM(98)102 (February 25, 1998), as well as the Council resolution on measures to address the Year 2000 computer problem at OJ No. C200/2 (July 15, 1999).

[34] See also the Commission statement at OJ No. C118/18 (April 29, 1999) and their press-release IP(98)1054 (December 12, 1998).

- Consulting extensively with other public and private sector organizations on main priorities, appropriate roles, and coordination in areas with significant cross-border effects such as energy, finance, telecommunications, and transport.

In the event, the anticipated problems largely failed to materialize, certainly due in part to the extensive preparations which were made. European authorities and their counterparts around the world continued to monitor the situation after the transitional date on a stand-by basis.[35]

[35] Commission press-release IP(00)1 (January 4, 2000).

CHAPTER 4

EXTERNAL TRADE RELATIONS

International trade in information technology is helping to accelerate the integration of the global economy by making sophisticated, high quality, and competitively priced items available worldwide. In recent years, the centerpiece has been the Information Technology Agreement, under the auspices of the World Trade Organization (WTO), which provides for the gradual elimination of tariffs over a specified period. Other important Community regulation covers strategic export controls for dual-use products, customs legislation, and commercial policy measures to ensure fair trade practices. Each of these areas is discussed in detail in the sections that follow.

1. International Arrangements

1.1. World Trade Organization

At the multilateral level, the Community is party to the agreements resulting from the Uruguay Round negotiations for establishment of the WTO.[1] For information technology, important provisions cover trade in goods and services, elimination of technical barriers, rules of origin, trade-related investment measures (TRIMs), and trade-related aspects of intellectual property rights (TRIPs). Specific items will be referenced as appropriate in other sections.

1.2. Information Technology Agreement

As an outgrowth of the WTO, the EU and other members comprising approximately 90% of global trade in electronics entered into an Information Technology Agreement (ITA) for the phased reduction and complete elimination of import duties on a broad range of products between July 1997 and the year 2000.[2] In addition, the Community and the U.S. accelerated the removal of tariffs on certain semiconductors and other items in advance of the timetable prescribed by the ITA.[3] Within the EU, these measures are being implemented

---

1 Council Decision No. 94/800 concerning the conclusion on behalf of the European Community, as regards matters within its competence, of the agreements reached in the Uruguay Round multilateral negotiations (1986–1994), OJ No. L336/1 (December 23, 1994).

2 Council Decision No. 97/359 concerning the elimination of duties on information technology products, OJ No. L155/1 (June 12, 1997). This contains a comprehensive listing of products along with detailed schedules for implementation.

3 This helped pave the way for European companies to become full participants in the World Semiconductor Council. See Commission press-release IP(97)182 (March 5, 1997).

by amendments to the Common Customs Tariff as described at Section 3.2 of this Chapter below.

1.3. Mutual Recognition

Consistent with the WTO agreement on technical barriers to trade,[4] the Community has negotiated bilateral arrangements with a number of countries for the mutual recognition of conformity assessment which enable products tested and approved in one jurisdiction to be sold in the other without additional certification procedures.[5] These include telecommunications terminal equipment, electrical safety, and electromagnetic compatibility. The agreements are structured as framework texts which permit extension to other sectors as appropriate.

2. Strategic Export Controls

Since July 1995, the Community has operated an integrated system of export controls for strategic products with both civilian and military applications based on Council Regulation No. 3381/94[6] and Council Decision No. 94/942/CFSP.[7] These rules form part of the common foreign and security policy and are without prejudice to the normal provisions in the Community Customs Code at Section 3 below.[8]

Article 3(1) of Regulation No. 3381/94 establishes the basic requirement that authorization is necessary for export of the dual-use items listed in Annex I of Decision No. 94/942/CFSP.[9] Under Annex I, information technology is covered by categories 3–5 for electronics, computers, and telecommunications and information security, respectively. Within each category, there is an additional breakdown comprising:

– Equipment, assemblies, and components,

---

4 See OJ No. L336/86 (December 23, 1994).

5 For example, see Council Decisions No. 98/566 and No. 1999/78 on conclusion of agreements for mutual recognition with Canada and the U.S. at OJ No. L280/1 (October 16, 1998) and OJ No. L31/1 (February 4, 1999), respectively. See also the Council resolution on the management of agreements for mutual recognition, OJ No. C190/2 (July 7, 1999). This is distinct from the principle of mutual recognition designed to promote free movement of goods in the EU internal market discussed at Section 5.1 of Chapter 2.

6 Council Regulation No. 3381/94 setting up a Community regime for the control of exports of dual-use goods, OJ No. L367/1 (December 31, 1994), as amended by Council Regulation No. 837/95, OJ No. L90/1 (April 21, 1995).

7 Council Decision No. 94/942/CFSP on the joint action adopted by the Council on the basis of Article J.3 of the EU Treaty concerning the control of exports of dual-use goods, OJ No. L367/8 (December 31, 1994), as amended at OJ No. L90/2 (April 21, 1995). Detailed revisions to the technical Annexes in Decision No. 94/942/CFSP appear at OJ No. L90/3 (April 21, 1995), OJ No. L278/1 (October 30, 1996), OJ No. L178/1 (July 7, 1997), OJ No. L266/1 (September 29, 1997), OJ No. L32/1 (February 6, 1998), OJ No. L92/1 (March 25, 1998), OJ No. L18/1 (January 23, 1999), OJ No. L73/1 (March 19, 1999), and OJ No. L82/1 (April 1, 2000).

8 See the preamble and Article 2(b) of Regulation No. 3381/94.

9 If the appropriate conditions are met, authorization may also be required for the export of certain dual-use items not listed in Annex I. See Articles 3(2), 4, and 5 of Regulation No. 3381/94.

- Test, inspection, and production equipment,
- Materials, software, and technology.

Authorization is granted by the Member State where the exporter is established in accordance with common guidelines reflecting international obligations, considerations of national foreign and security policy, and the intended end-use and risk of diversion of the relevant item.[10] Depending on the circumstances, approval may be individual, general, or global.[11] Exporters are expected to keep detailed records of transactions, while Member States are responsible for ensuring proper enforcement through effective, proportionate, and dissuasive penalties.[12]

A pending proposal from the Commission would supersede Regulation No. 3381/94 but leave the system essentially intact, including the list of product categories in Annex I,[13] with the following modifications:

- It would expressly extend to dual-use technology exported by electronic media, fax, and telephone.[14]
- Regular updating of controlled items would be delegated to a special List Group and incorporated as amendments to Annex I by Commission regulation.[15]

3. Community Customs Code

The Community Customs Code prescribes the general requirements for trade in goods between the EU and third countries.[16] It is implemented by the Commission[17] and is without prejudice to other specific legislation such as the commercial policy measures at Section 4 below.[18] Under Article 20(3) of the Code, the Community customs tariff comprises the combined nomenclature (CN) of goods, non-preferential tariffs, autonomous

---

10 Articles 7 and 8 of Regulation No. 3381/94 and Annex III of Decision No. 94/942/CFSP.

11 Article 6 of Regulation No. 3381/94 and Annex II of Decision No. 94/942/CFSP.

12 Articles 14 and 17 of Regulation No. 3381/94.

13 Commission proposal for a Council Regulation setting up a Community regime for the control of exports of dual-use goods and technology, OJ No. C399/1 (December 21, 1998).

14 Articles 1, 2(a)–(c), and 3(2) of the Commission proposal at note 13 above.

15 Article 12 of the Commission proposal at note 13 above.

16 Council Regulation No. 2913/92 establishing the Community Customs Code, OJ No. L302/1 (October 19, 1992), as amended by Regulation No. 82/97 of the European Parliament and Council, OJ No. L17/1 (January 21, 1997), and Regulation No. 955/1999 of the European Parliament and Council, OJ No. L119/1 (May 7, 1999).

17 Commission Regulation No. 2454/93 laying down provisions for the implementation of Council Regulation No. 2913/92 establishing the Community Customs Code, OJ No. L253/1 (October 11, 1993). The numerous detailed amendments to Regulation No. 2454/93 appear at OJ No. L335/1 (December 31, 1993), OJ No. L82/15 (March 25, 1994), OJ No. L162/1 (June 30, 1994), OJ No. L235/6 (September 9, 1994), OJ No. L346/1 (December 31, 1994), OJ No. L171/8 (July 21, 1995), OJ No. L70/4 (March 20, 1996), OJ No. L218/1 (August 28, 1996), OJ No. L289/1 (November 12, 1996), OJ No. L9/1 (January 13, 1997) ,OJ No. L17/28 (January 21, 1997), OJ No. L196/31 (July 24, 1997), OJ No. L7/3 (January 13, 1998), OJ No. L212/18 (July 30, 1998), OJ No. L10/1 (January 15, 1999), OJ No. L65/1 (March 12, 1999), and OJ No. L197/25 (July 29, 1999).

18 See the preamble and Article 1 of Regulation No. 2913/92.

duty suspensions, and other items. These subjects, as well as related issues on the classification and origin of goods, are discussed in the sections that follow.

3.1. Combined Nomenclature

Council Regulation No. 2658/87 establishes the CN which contains the basic classification of goods and rates of duty for tariff purposes.[19] Annex I of the Regulation has a comprehensive listing of individual products including information technology categorized by CN code or sub-heading. Under Article 12, the Commission is required to publish a complete new version annually which becomes effective in the following January. The CN is supplemented by the integrated tariff of the European Communities (Taric) which designates additional sub-headings for items such as duty suspensions, quotas, tariff preferences, and antidumping or countervailing duties.[20] Taken together, the CN, rates of duty, and measures included in the Taric or other arrangements constitute the common customs tariff (CCT) which applies to the import of goods into the Community.[21]

3.2. Non-Preferential Tariffs

These are the autonomous and conventional rates of duty which are included with the CN in Annex I of Regulation No. 2658/87. For selected information technology products, the rates are gradually being eliminated in accordance with the ITA discussed at Section 1.2 above. The initial reductions were made in 1997.[22] Since then, the changes have been incorporated in the Commission's annual revisions to Annex I of Regulation No. 2658/87.[23] The products covered by the ITA appear at their respective CN codes or sub-headings in the following general categories of the CN:

- Chapter 38: chemical elements and compounds for use in electronics.
- Chapter 70: certain articles of glass including quartz reactor tubes and holders designed for diffusion and oxidation furnaces in the production of semiconductor wafers.
- Chapter 84: machinery and mechanical appliances.
- Chapter 85: electrical machinery and equipment.
- Chapter 90: photographic, optical, measuring, and other apparatus.

---

19 Council Regulation No. 2658/87 on the tariff and statistical nomenclature and the Common Customs Tariff, OJ No. L256/1 (September 7, 1987), as amended by Council Regulation No. 254/2000, OJ No. L28/16 (February 3, 2000). See also the explanatory notes to the CN as last published at OJ No. C287/1 (September 15, 1998).

20 Article 2 of Regulation No. 2658/87. The most recent version of the Taric is published at OJ No. C115/1 (April 25, 2000).

21 Article 4 of Regulation No. 2658/87.

22 See Council Regulation No. 2216/97, OJ No. L305/1 (November 8, 1997) and Commission Regulation No. 1153/97, OJ No. L168/35 (June 26, 1997).

23 See Commission Regulation No. 2204/1999, OJ No. L278/1 (October 28, 1999), Commission Regulation No. 2261/98, OJ No. L292/1 (October 30, 1998), and Commission Regulation No. 2086/97, OJ No. L312/1 (November 14, 1997).

3.3. *Preferential Tariffs*

In addition to the rates in the preceding section, the Community applies various preferential tariffs which provide reduced or duty-free treatment for imports from certain developing countries. The most comprehensive is the generalized system of preferences (GSP).[24] Under Council Regulation No. 2820/98, this has been extended through December 2001.[25] Articles 1 and 2 and Annex I of the Regulation list the products covered and the schedules for reduction or elimination of duties. The eligible beneficiary countries are in Annex III, along with a sub-category in Annex IV for the least-developed which qualify for special support arrangements. There is also a "graduation mechanism" for the removal of beneficiaries in accordance with prescribed criteria for development including per-capita gross national product.[26]

3.4. *Duty Suspension*

Finally, there are provisions for the total or partial suspension of customs duties on selected products including information technology.[27] Depending on the circumstances, this may be for an unlimited quantity or in accordance with a prescribed quota. In each case, the rationale for the suspension is that intra-Community production of the relevant items is insufficient to meet the requirements of European user industries.

3.5. *Tariff Classification*

To determine the applicable customs treatment and rate of duty, it is essential to identify the correct tariff classification for the particular product in the combined nomenclature.[28] In doubtful cases, the primary method is to apply to EU customs authorities for "binding tariff information" (BTI).[29] In addition, the Commission periodically issues regulations on

---

[24] Council Regulation No. 3281/94 applying a four-year scheme of generalized tariff preferences (1995–1998) in respect of certain industrial products originating in developing countries, OJ No. L348/1 (December 31, 1994), with corrigenda at OJ No. L82/29 (April 12, 1995). The detailed technical annexes to the Regulation were amended at OJ No. L308/32 (December 21, 1995), OJ No. L333/10 (December 21, 1996), OJ No. L144/13 (June 4, 1997), and OJ No. L80/1 (March 18, 1998).

[25] Council Regulation No. 2820/98 applying a multiannual scheme of generalized tariff preferences for the period July 1, 1999 to December 31, 2001, OJ No. L357/1 (December 30, 1998).

[26] Articles 1(4) and 3–5 of Regulation No. 2820/98.

[27] Council Regulation No. 1255/96 temporarily suspending the autonomous Common Customs Tariff duties on certain industrial and agricultural products, OJ No. L158/1 (June 29, 1996), as last amended at OJ No. L8/1 (January 12, 2000), and Council Regulation No. 2505/96 opening and providing for the administration of Community tariff quotas for certain agricultural and industrial products, OJ No. L345/1 (December 31, 1996), as last amended at OJ No. L331/17 (December 23, 1999). See also the Commission communication concerning autonomous tariff suspensions and quotas at OJ No. C128/2 (April 25, 1998).

[28] See Article 20 of Regulation No. 2913/92, as amended, at note 16 above.

[29] Article 12 of Regulation No. 2913/92, as amended, at note 16 above. The detailed procedures for issuance of BTI are in Articles 5–15 and Annex 1 of Regulation No. 2454/93, cited at note 17 above, as amended by Regulation No. 12/97, OJ No. L9/1 (January 13, 1997).

classification in consultation with the Tariff and Statistical Nomenclature section of the Customs Code Committee. Selected examples for information technology cover CD-ROM drives and tuner cards for multimedia operations, laptop computers with built-in programs for arithmetic and other purposes, microprocessor (smart) card readers, and multifunctional apparatus for operating as copier, fax, printer, and scanner within a computer network.[30]

The Court of Justice has also interpreted the CN in cases involving diverse items such as image processors, modules with disk drives, analog-to-digital converters, and silicon wafers for the manufacture of integrated circuits.[31]

In 1998, a WTO appellate panel upheld the EU on a complaint by the U.S. concerning the tariff classification of computer local area network (LAN) equipment.[32] These products were originally placed in a lower tariff category by Ireland and the United Kingdom, but were subsequently reclassified to a higher category throughout the EU. The U.S. claimed a legitimate expectation that the prior situation in Ireland and the U.K. would continue, but the WTO ruled that reclassification was consistent with EU international obligations under the GATT. According to the EU, this affirms the principle that they constitute a customs union comprising a single export market and not a collection of individual Member States.

3.6. Origin of Goods

As with tariff classification, determining the origin of goods is critical for customs and related purposes.

The basic framework is established by the WTO agreement on rules of origin.[33] For non-preferential trade, the relevant provisions are in Articles 22–26 of Council Regulation No. 2913/92.[34] Article 23 applies to goods wholly produced in one country. For two or more countries, Article 24 prescribes the place of the "last, substantial, economically justified processing or working ... resulting in the manufacture of a new product or representing an important stage of manufacture." In practice, this involves a change of tariff classification, minimum *ad valorem* percentage, or specified manufacturing or processing operation.[35]

---

[30] See Commission Regulation No. 517/1999, OJ No. L61/23 (March 10, 1999); Commission Regulation No. 981/98, OJ No. L137/9 (May 9, 1998); and Commission Regulation No. 2564/95, OJ No. L262/25 (November 1, 1995). See also Commission Regulation No. 936/1999 amending or repealing certain regulations on the classification of goods in the CN, OJ No. L117/9 (May 5, 1999).

[31] See, respectively, *Techex Computer v. Hauptzollamt Muenchen*, Case No. C-382/95, OJ No. C55/10 (February 20, 1998), 1997 ECR I-7363; *Vobis Microcomputer v. Oberfinanzdirektion Muenchen*, Case No. C-121/95, OJ No. C336/1 (November 11, 1996), 1996 ECR I-3047; *Hauptzollamt Muenchen-West v. Analog Devices*, Case No. C-467/93, OJ No. C189/3 (July 22, 1995), 1995 ECR I-1403; and *Directeur Général des Douanes et des Droits Indirects v. Powerex Europe*, Case No. C-66/89, 1990 ECR I-1959, 1991-2 CMLR 529.

[32] Commission press-release IP(98)510 (June 5, 1998).

[33] OJ No. L336/144 (December 23, 1994).

[34] See note 16 above. Procedures for implementation are in Articles 35–65 and Annexes 9–13 of Commission Regulation No. 2454/93 at note 17 above.

[35] See Articles 2(a) and 9(2)(c) of the WTO agreement on rules of origin at note 33 above. For the judicial approach to assembly operations, see *Brother International v. Hauptzollamt Giessen*, Case No. C-26/88,

In addition, eligibility for preferential tariffs requires compliance with the appropriate definition of origin.[36] This is covered by Article 27 of Council Regulation No. 2913/92 as implemented by Articles 66–140 and Annexes 14–22 of Commission Regulation No. 2454/93.[37]

Finally, special rules on origin may be adopted in connection with commercial policy measures as discussed at Section 4.[38]

As with BTI, customs authorities are empowered to issue "binding origin information" (BOI) for both preferential and non-preferential trade.[39] The Commission has also issued special interpretive regulations applicable to a number of electronics products as follows:

- *Integrated circuits*: origin based on the operation of diffusion where circuits are formed on a semiconductor substrate by the selective introduction of an appropriate dopant.[40]
- *Photocopiers*: origin may *not* be based on assembly accompanied by manufacture of the harness, drum, rollers, side plates, roller bearings, screws, and nuts.[41]
- *Radios, television receivers, and tape recorders*: origin based on a specified percentage of the ex-factory invoice price.[42]

4. Commercial Policy Measures

4.1. Antidumping and Countervailing Duties

Community legislation calls for antidumping or countervailing duties to be applied to any dumped or subsidized product whose release for free circulation causes injury.[43] In each case, this covers material injury or threat of injury to a Community industry, along with

1989 ECR 4253, 1990-3 CMLR 658. This deals with prior legislation containing the same language as Article 24 of Regulation No. 2913/92.

36 For example, see Article 1(5) of Regulation No. 2820/98 at note 25 above.

37 See citations at notes 16 and 17 above. Relevant amendments to Regulation No. 2454/93 appear at OJ No. L335/1 (December 31, 1993), OJ No. L346/1 (December 31, 1994), OJ No. L9/1 (January 13, 1997), and OJ No. L10/1 (January 15, 1999).

38 Article 14(3) of Council Regulation No. 384/96 and Article 24(3) of Council Regulation No. 2026/97 at note 43 below.

39 See citations at note 29 above.

40 Commission Regulation No. 288/89 on determining the origin of integrated circuits, OJ No. L33/23 (February 4, 1989).

41 Commission Regulation No. 2071/89 on determining the origin of photocopying apparatus incorporating an optical system or of the contact type, OJ No. L196/24 (July 12, 1989). Compare Articles 2(f) and 9(1)(g) of the WTO agreement on rules of origin, cited at note 33 above, which generally discourage use of a "negative standard" except for purposes of clarification.

42 Commission Regulation No. 2632/70 on determining the origin of radio and television receivers, OJ No. L279/35 (December 24, 1970), and Commission Regulation No. 861/71 on determining the origin of tape recorders, OJ No. L95/11 (April 28, 1971).

43 Article 1(1) of Council Regulation No. 384/96 on protection against dumped imports from countries not members of the EC, OJ No. L56/1 (March 6, 1996), as amended by Council Regulation No. 905/98, OJ No. L128/18 (April 30, 1998), and Article 1(1) of Council Regulation No. 2026/97 on protection against subsidized imports from countries not members of the EC, OJ No. L288/1 (October 21, 1997). See also the Commission guidelines for the calculation of the amount of subsidy in countervailing duty investigations,

material retardation to the establishment of such an industry.[44] Once initiated, proceedings may be terminated without protective measures if appropriate, or with the imposition of definitive duties should the Community interest so require.[45] Concerned exporters may also offer voluntary undertakings to revise their commercial practices in order to eliminate the injury from the dumping or subsidy.[46] Measures normally expire after five years unless this would lead to continuation or recurrence of the dumping or subsidy and resulting injury.[47] Products may not be subject to both antidumping and countervailing duties arising from the same situation.[48]

Significant antidumping cases in recent years include the following products in the information technology sector:

- *DRAMs*: in 1990, a definitive duty of 60% was applied to imports of electronic integrated circuits known as dynamic random-access memories (DRAMs) originating in Japan.[49] This was accompanied by price undertakings from the major Japanese exporters who were accordingly exempt from the duty.[50] Additional measures comprising a duty of 24.7% and related undertakings were extended to imports from South Korea in 1993.[51] Due to a change in market conditions, these arrangements were suspended from June 1995 to March 1997.[52] After a thorough administrative review, the proceedings were eventually terminated without further protective measures in anticipation of voluntary industry agreements between the European, Japanese, and Korean producers aimed at preventing future dumping and ensuring that any new investigation would be carried out expeditiously.[53] The resulting agreements were subsequently approved by the Commission under the competition rules of the Treaty.[54]
- *EPROMs*: this was a companion case to DRAMs involving electronic integrated circuits known as erasable, programmable, read-only memories (EPROMs). A duty of

---

OJ No. C394/6 (December 17, 1998). These remedies are authorized by the WTO agreement on implementation of Article VI of the GATT 1994, OJ No. L336/103 (December 23, 1994), and the WTO agreement on subsidies and countervailing measures, OJ No. L336/156 (December 23, 1994).

44 Article 3 of Regulation No. 384/96 and Article 8 of Regulation No. 2026/97.

45 Articles 9(2), 9(4), and 21 of Regulation No. 384/96 and Articles 14(1), 15(1), and 31 of Regulation No. 2026/97.

46 Article 8(1) of Regulation No. 384/96 and Article 13(1) of Regulation No. 2026/97.

47 Article 11(2) of Regulation No. 384/96 and Article 18(1) of Regulation No. 2026/97.

48 Article 14(1) of Regulation No. 384/96 and Article 24(1) of Regulation No. 2026/97.

49 Council Regulation No. 2112/90, OJ No. L193/1 (July 25, 1990), as amended by Council Regulation No. 3049/90, OJ No. L292/16 (October 24, 1990), and Council Regulation No. 2967/92, OJ No. L299/4 (October 15, 1992).

50 Commission Regulation No. 165/90, OJ No. L20/5 (January 25, 1990), and Commission Decision No. 92/494, OJ No. L299/43 (October 15, 1992). See also Commission press-release IP(90)57 (January 23, 1990).

51 Council Regulation No. 611/93, OJ No. L66/1 (March 18, 1993), and Commission Decision No. 93/157, OJ No. L66/37 (March 18, 1993). See also Commission memorandum M-93/12 (March 16, 1993).

52 See Commission Decision No. 95/197, OJ No. L126/58 (June 9, 1995), Council Regulation No. 399/96, OJ No. L55/1 (March 6, 1996), and Commission press-release IP(97)198 (March 10, 1997).

53 Council Regulation No. 2335/97, OJ No. L324/11 (November 27, 1997), and Commission Decision No. 97/798, OJ No. L324/38 (November 27, 1997).

54 See the Commission notices at OJ No. C378/5-6 (December 13, 1997) and OJ No. C156/10 (May 21, 1998), and Commission press-releases IP(98)228 (March 10, 1998) and IP(98)896 (October 15, 1998).

94% was imposed on imports from Japan in 1991.[55] Undertakings were accepted from the Japanese exporters.[56] As with DRAMs, measures were suspended from mid-1995 due to market conditions.[57] The proceeding was terminated in 1997 based on the finding of no injury or likely recurrence of injury.[58]

- *Large electrolytic aluminum capacitors*: these are components used in most electronic equipment including consumer durables such as personal computers. Definitive duties of 75% were applied to imports from Japan in 1992, and from South Korea and Taiwan at the respective rates of 70.6% and 75.8% in 1994.[59] Additionally, provisional duties of 24.6% and 39.4% were assessed against products from the U.S. and Thailand.[60] Following detailed reviews, the proceedings were terminated without further protective measures in January 2000.[61]
- *Magnetic disks*: definitive duties ranging from 8.1 to 46.4% on 3.5" microdisks used to record and store encoded digital computer information imported from Hong Kong, Indonesia, Japan, Malaysia, Mexico, the People's Republic of China (PRC), South Korea, Taiwan, and the U.S.[62] An investigation into possible circumvention of the duties was terminated without further protective measures since there was no evidence of transshipments or the volume of imports was below the level normally regarded as negligible.[63]

---

[55] Council Regulation No. 557/91, OJ No. L65/1 (March 12, 1991), as amended by Council Regulation No. 2860/93, OJ No. L262/1 (October 21, 1993). See also Commission press-release IP(91)216 (March 12, 1991).

[56] Commission Decision No. 91/131, OJ No. L65/42 (March 12, 1991), and Commission Decision No. 93/538, OJ No. L262/64 (October 21, 1993).

[57] Commission Decision No. 95/272, OJ No. L165/26 (July 15, 1995), and Council Regulation No. 664/96, OJ No. L92/4 (April 13, 1996).

[58] Commission Decision No. 97/251, OJ No. L99/16 (April 16, 1997). Certain products known as Flash EPROMs were included in the agreements between European, Korean, and Japanese producers which were approved by the Commission under the competition rules as indicated at note 54 above.

[59] Council Regulation No. 3842/92, OJ No. L353/1 (December 3, 1992), and Council Regulation No. 1384/94, OJ No. L152/1 (June 18, 1994).

[60] Commission Regulation No. 1845/98, OJ No. L240/4 (August 28, 1998).

[61] See Council Regulation No. 173/2000, OJ No. L22/1 (January 27, 2000), which applies to Japan, South Korea, and Taiwan. This was done in order to avoid unfair discrimination with the U.S. and Thailand since protective measures on imports from those countries lapsed in February 1999 when the Council failed to adopt definitive duties within the prescribed period.

[62] Council Regulation No. 2861/93, OJ No. L262/4 (October 21, 1993); Council Regulation No. 2199/94, OJ No. L236/2 (September 10, 1994); Council Regulation No. 663/96, OJ No. L92/1 (April 13, 1996); and Council Regulation No. 1821/98, OJ No. L236/1 (August 22, 1998). The duties applicable to Hong Kong, South Korea, Japan, Taiwan, and the PRC are currently under review. See OJ No. C322/4 (October 21, 1998), OJ No. C181/21 (June 26, 1999), and OJ No. C256/3 (September 9, 1999). By Council Regulation No. 2537/1999, OJ No. L307/1 (December 2, 1999), the product scope of these proceedings was amended to exclude microdisks based on optically continuous or magnetic sector servo-tracking technology with a storage capacity of 120 megabytes or more.

[63] Commission Regulation No. 1445/96, OJ No. L186/14 (July 25, 1996). A subsequent inquiry on alleged circumvention concerning products from Taiwan and the PRC was also terminated for non-compliance with the relevant standards. See Commission Regulation No. 799/2000, OJ No. L96/30 (April 18, 2000).

- *Printers*: duties of 47.0% and 23.5% on dot-matrix and daisywheel printers from Japan.[64] For the dot-matrix type, the product definition excluded certain special purpose printers, hand-held portable printers, and printers imported and sold as integral parts of a computer system. These measures expired in November 1993 and January 1994.[65]

4.2. *Safeguards*

Safeguard mechanisms for quantitative restrictions come into play when imports of a particular product cause or threaten serious injury to Community producers.[66] The focus is on volume and price including the consequent impact on European production, capacity utilization, inventories, sales, market share, profits, return on capital, cash flow, and employment.[67] If appropriate, procedures for Community surveillance of the relevant items may lead to quotas or other measures to limit imports.[68] The maximum initial duration is four years which may be extended as necessary to a total of eight years in order to give the Community industry a reasonable period to adjust.[69]

4.3. *Unfair Trade Practices*

Council Regulation No. 3286/94 promotes exercise of the Community's rights under international law by authorizing a response to proscribed trade barriers with a view toward removing the resulting injury.[70] Article 2(1) defines "obstacles to trade" as any third country practice either prohibited by international rules or where there is a right for injured parties to seek elimination of an adverse effect. Detailed procedures are in Articles 3–8 with the relevant injury factors specified in Article 10. Sanctions may only be adopted after completion of required dispute-settlement mechanisms and in accordance with the results.[71] Potential remedies include suspension or withdrawal of concessions, tariff increases, quantitative restrictions, or other actions modifying conditions of trade with the third country concerned.[72]

---

64 Council Regulation No. 3651/88, OJ No. L317/33 (November 24, 1988), and Council Regulation No. 34/89, OJ No. L5/23 (January 7, 1989).

65 See Commission notices at OJ No. C311/5 (November 17, 1993) and OJ No. C344/4 (December 22, 1993).

66 Council Regulation No. 3285/94 on the common rules for imports and repealing Regulation No. 518/94, OJ No. L349/53 (December 31, 1994). These provisions are consistent with the WTO agreement on safeguards at OJ No. L336/184 (December 23, 1994).

67 Articles 5 and 10 of Regulation No. 3285/94.

68 Articles 11, 16, and 17 of Regulation No. 3285/94.

69 Article 20 of Regulation No. 3285/94.

70 See Article 1 of Council Regulation No. 3286/94 laying down Community procedures in the field of the common commercial policy in order to ensure the exercise of the Community's rights under international trade rules, in particular those established under the auspices of the WTO, OJ No. L349/71 (December 31, 1994), as amended by Council Regulation No. 356/95, OJ No. L41/3 (February 23, 1995).

71 Articles 12(1) and (2) of Regulation No. 3286/94 as amended.

72 Article 12(3) of Regulation No. 3286/94 as amended.

4.4. Counterfeit Goods

Finally, Council Regulation No. 3295/94 prohibits the unlawful trade in products which infringe certain intellectual property rights including counterfeit or pirated goods.[73] Article 3 of the Regulation prescribes the requirements for submission of a written application by the rightholder to customs authorities. Under Article 4, customs may detain suspect goods for a period of three working days on their own intiviative in order to notify the rightholder. The application is then forwarded to the agency in the Member State competent to make a substantive decision.[74] Illegal goods are destroyed, disposed of outside normal commercial channels, or otherwise handled so as to deprive the infringer of the economic benefits of the transaction.[75] Upon request, customs may also advise the rightholder of the quantities involved as well as the identities of the manufacturer, consignor, and importer or exporter of the infringing product.[76]

---

[73] Council Regulation No. 3295/94 laying down measures concerning the entry into the Community and the export and re-export from the Community of goods infringing certain intellectual property rights, OJ No. L341/8 (December 30, 1994), as amended by Council Regulation No. 241/1999, OJ No. L27/1 (February 2, 1999). These rules are consistent with Article 51 et seq. of the WTO agreement on trade-related aspects of intellectual property rights, OJ No. L336/213 (December 23, 1994), and are implemented by Commission Regulation No. 1367/95, OJ No. L133/2 (June 17, 1995) as amended by Commission Regulation No. 2549/1999, OJ No. L308/16 (December 3, 1999). See also note 3 at Chapter 6 below.

[74] Article 6 of Regulation No. 3295/94 as amended.

[75] Article 8(1) of Regulation No. 3295/94 as amended.

[76] Article 8(3) of Regulation No. 3295/94 as amended.

CHAPTER 5

COMPETITION POLICY

Competition policy has pervasive implications for all aspects of information technology including research and development, intellectual property, and the manufacture and distribution of goods and services. A detailed treatise on the subject is beyond the scope of this book, but the sections below cover the essential principles and procedures in each of the major areas: restriction of competition, abuse of a dominant position, mergers and joint ventures, and state aid to commercial enterprises.

In addition, to demonstrate how the policy actually works, the Appendix at Section 6 of this chapter summarizes selected cases which illustrate the application of the rules to specific representative transactions in the information technology sector. These are referenced as appropriate in the following text and highlight the significant underlying circumstances as well as the reasons for the particular outcome in each situation.

1. General: Articles 81 and 82[1]

1.1. Article 81: Restriction of Competition

Article 81(1) of the Treaty prohibits agreements and concerted practices which have the object or effect of restricting competition within the common market. This expressly includes those which:

- Directly or indirectly fix prices or other trading conditions.
- Limit or control production, markets, technical development, or investment.
- Share markets or sources of supply.
- Place other parties at a competitive disadvantage by applying dissimilar conditions to equivalent transactions.
- Make contracts subject to the acceptance of supplementary obligations which are unrelated by their nature or commercial usage.

Under Article 81(2), these prohibited practices are automatically void. However, Article 81(3) permits an exemption for restrictions which may improve production or distribution, promote technical or economic progress, and benefit consumers as long as they are indispensable to achieving the positive results and do not threaten to substantially eliminate competition. The procedures for exemption are discussed in Sections 2.2 and 3 below.

---

[1] These were formerly Articles 85 and 86, respectively, before the consolidation and renumbering prescribed by the Amsterdam Treaty. The text of each provision remains the same. For clarity, the current numbers will be substituted for the earlier versions throughout.

1.2. Article 82: Abuse of Dominant Position

Article 82 prohibits any abuse of a dominant position within the common market which may affect trade between Member States. Dominance is essentially a factual issue involving sufficient economic power to prevent effective competition on the relevant market.[2] The enumerated criteria for abuse are similar to the restrictions in Article 81 above. However, Article 82 may be violated by a single firm rather than two or more parties acting in concert, and there is no possibility of an exemption for prohibited practices.

2. Procedures: Articles 81 and 82

2.1. Notices and Communications

The Commission periodically issues notices, communications, and other published statements providing general guidance on the application of Articles 81 and 82 in important areas such as the methodology for determining the relevant product and geographic markets in competition investigations.[3] With specific reference to information technology, they have underscored the additional complexity for economic analysis arising from the convergence with telecommunications and the media discussed at Section 2 of Chapter 3 above:

> Defining markets and identifying the key factors governing competition are a permanent challenge to competition policy, particularly in markets which are in a state of rapid transition. A changing environment in which technological innovation is blurring the traditional distinctions between the various product markets (as is the case, in the "information society", with the boundaries between the information technology, telecommunications, and media markets), promoting the emergence of new markets whose geographical boundaries are similarly in a state of flux, places increased demands on the Commission and its staff in terms of economic analysis. This applies particularly to market definition, the analysis of market power, the taking into account of potential competition, and more generally the economic assessment called for under Article 81(3).[4]

Other comments have focused on the interplay between competition policy and intellectual property in relation to computer software, with an emphasis on the extension of

---

[2] This is based on factors such as the strength and number of competitors, relative market shares, technological capabilities, potential competition, barriers to entry, and so on. Compare the discussion on the Merger Control Regulation at Section 4.3 below.

[3] See OJ No. C372/5 (December 9, 1997). Other examples include the method for establishing the amount of fines for violations of the competition rules, OJ No. C9/3 (January 14, 1998); *de minimis* agreements which are not restrictive of competition since their effects are considered negligible, OJ No. C372/13 (December 9, 1997); the role of national competition authorities in applying the rules, OJ No. C313/3 (October 15, 1997); right of access to the investigative file, OJ No. C23/3 (January 23, 1997); reduction of fines for companies cooperating in investigations, OJ No. C207/4 (July 18, 1996); and the respective functions of the Commission and national courts under Articles 81 and 82, OJ No. C39/6 (February 13, 1993).

[4] Part One of the European Commission 26th Report on Competition Policy 1996 at ¶13.

copyright for interfaces and the risk that access to unprotected parts of a program might be legally blocked.[5] According to the Commission, there may be a prohibited restriction from any attempt to extend the scope of protection to uncopyrighted aspects of a program by contract or otherwise. Under appropriate circumstances, it could also be an abuse for a dominant firm to exercise intellectual property in order to deny competitors access to information necessary to write independent compatible software, or to use exclusive rights in one product to gain an unfair advantage in other unprotected items.[6]

2.2. Negative Clearance and Individual Exemption

The procedures for negative clearance and individual exemption are prescribed by Council Regulation No. 17/62 as amended.[7] A negative clearance is a declaration by the Commission that conduct is not prohibited by Article 81(1) or 82, while an exemption reflects compliance with the criteria in Article 81(3).[8]

Applications for negative clearance and notifications for exemption are submitted to the Commission on Form A/B in accordance with Commission Regulation No. 3385/94.[9] Upon notification, the parties receive immunity from fines for conduct within its scope pending the final outcome.[10] The decision by the Commission may be in either a formal ruling or "comfort letter".[11]

As the outgrowth of a recent policy review,[12] an amendment to Regulation No. 17/62 eliminates the need for prior notification in order to obtain individual exemption under Article 81(3) for "vertical" agreements between producers and distributors for the

---

5 European Commission 19th Report on Competition Policy 1989 at ¶34.

6 European Commission 18th Report on Competition Policy 1988 at ¶42. See also the Commission's proposal for a Council Directive on the legal protection of computer programs at ¶¶3.9–3.15 (access protocols and interfaces) of the explanatory memorandum (Part one) and "conclusions," OJ No. C91/4 (April 12, 1989). The EU Computer Software Directive is discussed at Section 2 of Chapter 6 below.

7 Council Regulation No. 17/62: first Regulation implementing Articles 81 and 82 of the Treaty, OJ No. 13/204 (February 21, 1962), as amended by Council Regulation No. 1216/1999, OJ No. L148/5 (June 15, 1999).

8 Articles 2 and 4 of Regulation No. 17/62. As indicated at Section 1.2 above, there is no exemption for abuse of a dominant position under Article 82.

9 Commission Regulation No. 3385/94 on the form, content, and other details of applications and notifications provided for in Council Regulation No. 17/62, OJ No. L377/28 (December 31, 1994). Form A/B calls for complete information and evidentiary support on the parties, their corporate groups, the arrangements being notified, relevant markets, potential competition, barriers to entry, and the reasons underlying the application for negative clearance or exemption.

10 Article 15 of Regulation No. 17/62. The Regulation contains detailed rules on the Commission's power to investigate, order termination of infringements, and impose sanctions for violations. See Articles 3, 11, and 14–17 of Regulation No. 17/62. See also Commission Decision No. 94/810 on the terms of reference for hearing officers in competition procedures before the Commission, OJ No. L330/67 (December 21, 1994), and Commission Regulation No. 2842/98 on the hearing of parties in certain proceedings under Articles 81 and 82 of the Treaty, OJ No. L354/18 (December 30, 1998).

11 See the Commission notice on procedures concerning notifications pursuant to Article 4 of Council Regulation No. 17/62, OJ No. C295/6 (November 2, 1983).

12 See the Commission communication on application of the Community competition rules to vertical restraints, OJ No. C365/3 (November 26, 1998).

purchase, sale, or resale of goods or services.[13] Other pending proposals for radical and far-reaching procedural reform would entirely abolish the long-standing requirement for individual notification and exemption by the Commission under Article 81(3) and instead make that provision directly applicable and subject to the national jurisdiction of the Member States.[14]

For an example of a decision under Article 81(1), see *STACK International* (Section 6.1.4) where the Commission determined that there was no restriction of competition from the activities of a non-profit organization which defined generic specifications for electronic components and certified compliance by products and manufacturers. Cases granting individual exemption in accordance with Article 81(3) include:

– Standard distribution franchise agreements for the sale of microcomputers from a wide range of different manufacturers to end-users in Europe (*Computerland*, Section 6.1.1).
– Joint venture to build and operate a plant in Japan for the production of new-generation integrated circuits (*Fujitsu AMD Semiconductor*, Section 6.1.2).
– Strategic alliance for the licensing of Alpha AXP technology based on RISC microprocessors (*Olivetti/Digital*, Section 6.1.3).
– Agreement among computer manufacturers to develop standard interface definitions for applications software to be used with the Unix operating system (*X/Open Group*, Section 6.1.6).

Finally, in *Systemform* the Commission imposed a fine for prohibited restrictions relating to export bans and resale prices in exclusive distribution arrangements (Section 6.1.5).

For the alleged abuse of a dominant position under Article 82, see the investigations involving:

– Exclusionary practices aimed at third-party maintenance providers in the markets for hardware and software services (*Digital*, Section 6.2.1).
– Withholding of critical interface information and other restrictions relating to System 370 computers (*IBM*, Section 6.2.2).
– Anticompetitive licensing agreements in the market for operating systems software for personal computers (*Microsoft*, Section 6.2.3).

2.3. Limitation Periods

Council Regulation No. 2988/74[15] establishes the following limitation periods for proceedings and the enforcement of sanctions under Articles 81 and 82:[16]

– Three years for infringements concerning applications or notifications, requests for information, or investigations.

---

[13] Council Regulation No. 1216/1999 cited at note 7 above. The purpose is to promote administrative simplicity and provide firms with greater legal certainty for qualified arrangements which meet the relevant criteria.

[14] See the summary at ¶¶3–16 of the Commission White Paper on modernization of the rules implementing Articles 81 and 82 of the Treaty, OJ No. C132/1 (May 12, 1999). The Commission would retain a leading role in establishing principles for the interpretation of Articles 81 and 82 through notices and block exemption regulations as well as decisions in major cases with a genuine Community interest. To ensure coherence and

– Five years for all other infringements.
– Five years for enforcement of decisions imposing fines, penalties, or periodic payments.

In each case, there are detailed rules for the commencement, interruption, and suspension of the relevant periods.[17]

2.4. *Judicial Review*

There are direct appeals from Commission decisions in competition cases, including the imposition of fines, in accordance with Articles 229 and 230 of the Treaty.[18] Intermediate appellate jurisdiction is in the Court of First Instance, with further review by the Court of Justice limited to points of law.[19] Under Article 234, the Court of Justice may also issue preliminary rulings interpreting competition questions in matters referred to it by the national courts of the Member States.[20]

3. Block Exemptions

These are regulations issued by the Commission, based on authority from the Council,[21] which automatically exempt certain enumerated practices without notification since they are considered compatible with Article 81(3). Typically, the regulations indicate what particular provisions may and may not be included in agreements between the parties in order to qualify.[22]

The block exemptions are complex and must be examined carefully in each situation to determine whether they might apply. They are not directed at information technology as such, but can nevertheless play a positive role in facilitating commercial transactions between firms in that industry engaged in the production and distribution of goods or

---

uniformity, national courts would be obliged to avoid conflict with EU policy and matters could be removed from local consideration if appropriate. Specific legislation to implement these recommendations is expected.

15 Council Regulation No. 2988/74 concerning limitation periods in proceedings and the enforcement of sanctions under the rules of the European Economic Community relating to transport and competition, OJ No. L319/1 (November 29, 1974).

16 Articles 1(1) and 4(1) of Regulation No. 2988/74.

17 Articles 1(2)–3 and 4(2)–6 of Regulation No. 2988/74.

18 These were formerly Articles 172 and 173 before the changes in the Amsterdam Treaty.

19 See Article 225 of the Treaty (former Article 168a) and Council Decision No. 93/350, OJ No. L144/21 (June 16, 1993).

20 Article 234 was formerly Article 177. Under Article 225, these preliminary references are expressly excluded from the jurisdiction of the Court of First Instance.

21 See Council Regulation No. 19/65 on the application of Article 81(3) of the Treaty to certain categories of agreements and concerted practices, OJ No. 36/533 (March 6, 1965), as amended by Council Regulation No. 1215/1999, OJ No. L148/1 (June 15, 1999).

22 Agreements with terms going beyond the scope of the regulations may still be exempted, but only upon individual notification as discussed at Section 2.2 above. In certain cases, the block exemption regulations may contain an "opposition procedure" for notification and accelerated approval of such agreements if the Commission does not object within a prescribed period.

services, research and development, or the transfer of intellectual property. The most important are summarized below.[23]

3.1. Distribution and Purchasing

The original block exemptions for exclusive distribution and purchasing were in Commission Regulations No. 1983/83 and No. 1984/83.[24] In addition to exclusivity, these permitted a degree of territorial protection coupled with obligations to purchase complete ranges or minimum quantities, sell products with trademarks or other appropriate packaging, take prescribed measures for sales promotion, and not manufacture or distribute competing goods.[25] These measures have now been replaced by Commission Regulation No. 2790/1999 on vertical agreements.[26] Articles 2(1) and 3 establish the basic exemption for arrangements between companies at different levels of production or distribution for the purchase, sale, or resale of goods or services provided that their market share does not exceed 30%. There is no presumption of illegality above that percentage but individual examination may be necessary. Under Article 2(4), vertical agreements between competitors are generally not exempted unless they comply with stringent turnover and other criteria. Detailed requirements for the calculation of market share and turnover are in Articles 9 and 10.

Regardless of market share, Article 4 prohibits exemption of agreements containing anticompetitive restrictions which fix resale prices or impose certain types of territorial and customer allocation. Under Article 5, other selected provisions including non-competition clauses may or may not be authorized depending on the circumstances. The Regulation does not apply to agreements subject to other block exemptions and is without prejudice to Article 82 on abuse of a dominant position.[27] To assist companies, the Commission has prepared a set of guidelines on vertical restraints which interpret the block exemption along with other practices going beyond its scope.[28]

---

23 This listing does not cover sectoral measures such as Commission Regulation No. 3652/93 on the application of Article 81(3) to certain categories of agreements relating to computerized reservation systems for air transport services, OJ No. 333/37 (December 31, 1993).

24 Commission Regulations No. 1983/83 and No. 1984/83 on the application of Article 81(3) of the Treaty to categories of exclusive distribution and exclusive purchasing agreements, OJ No. L173/1 and OJ No. L173/5 (June 30, 1983), respectively. For detailed guidance on the application of these measures, see the Commission notice at OJ No. C101/2 (April 13, 1984).

25 Articles 1 and 2(1)–(3) of Regulations No. 1983/83 and 1984/83, respectively.

26 Commission Regulation No. 2790/1999 on the application of Article 81(3) of the Treaty to categories of vertical agreements and concerted practices, OJ No. L336/21 (December 29, 1999). This also supersedes Commission Regulation No. 4087/88 on franchising at Section 3.2 below. Under Article 13, Regulation No. 2790/1999 becomes effective on June 1, 2000 and remains in force through May 31, 2010. Article 12 contains transitional provisions for the continued exemption of qualified pre-existing agreements under the old Regulations until December 31, 2001.

27 Article 2(5) and Recital 16 of Regulation No. 2790/1999.

28 See the Commission communication including draft guidelines on vertical restraints at OJ No. C270/7 (September 24, 1999). This has now been approved in final form but the definitive text has not yet appeared in the Official Journal. The draft guidelines contain comments on the appropriate treatment of computer software (¶¶33 and 34) and the use of the Internet for advertising and selling products (¶42).

3.2. Franchising

Commission Regulation No. 4087/88 exempted franchise agreements for the retailing of goods and services to end-users including relationships involving a third party (master franchisee).[29] In exchange for an exclusive territory, the franchisee could be prohibited from actively seeking customers outside that area and from selling or using competing goods.[30] The exemption was also extended to clauses which are essential for preserving the common identity and reputation of the network or preventing the know-how and assistance provided by the franchisor from benefiting competitors.[31] As with the block exemptions for exclusive distribution and purchasing, this is being replaced by Commission Regulation No. 2790/1999.[32]

3.3. Research and Development

Commission Regulation No. 418/85 provides an exemption for the cooperative research and development of products or processes including joint exploitation of the results.[33] This can be essential, even for firms with substantial resources, in view of the increasing start-up costs and diminishing life-cycles of many items in the information technology sector. Under Article 1(2)(d), exploitation covers manufacture of the contract products, application of contract processes, and the assignment or licensing of any resulting intellectual property and know-how. Permissible obligations include a degree of territorial protection, field-of-use restrictions, minimum quantity and quality requirements, procurement of contract products exclusively from designated parties, and joint distribution subject to certain market-share limitations.[34] The Regulation remains in effect through December 2000 when the Commission proposes to replace it with a simplified approach based on a combined market-share threshold of 25% for qualified arrangements.[35]

3.4. Specialization

Commission Regulation No. 417/85 encourages firms to collaborate in order to achieve efficiency gains by specializing in particular aspects of the production process.[36] Article 1

---

[29] Commission Regulation No. 4087/88 on the application of Article 81(3) of the Treaty to categories of franchise agreements, OJ No. L359/46 (December 28, 1988). See generally Articles 1(1)–(3) and Recitals 4 and 5 of Regulation No. 4087/88.

[30] Articles 2 (a)–(e) and Recital 9 of Regulation No. 4087/88.

[31] See Article 3 and Recital 11 of Regulation No. 4087/88.

[32] See Section 3.1 and notes 26–28 above.

[33] Commission Regulation No. 418/85 on the application of Article 81(3) of the Treaty to categories of research and development agreements, OJ No. L53/5 (February 22, 1985), as amended by Commission Regulation No. 151/93, OJ No. L21/8 (January 29, 1993), and Commission Regulation No. 2236/97, OJ No. L306/12 (November 11, 1997).

[34] See Articles 4 and 5 of Regulation No. 418/85 as amended.

[35] Article 13 of Regulation No. 418/85 as amended. For the Commission proposal, see their communication on competition rules relating to horizontal cooperation agreements, OJ No. C118/3 (April 27, 2000).

[36] Commission Regulation No. 417/85 on the application of Article 81(3) of the Treaty to categories of specialization agreements, OJ No. L53/1 (February 22, 1985), as amended by Commission Regulation No. 151/93,

exempts agreements with reciprocal obligations to allocate activities between the parties or manufacture certain items jointly. Other permissible restrictions are similar to those for research and development including joint distribution within prescribed limits for market share.[37] The Regulation is scheduled to expire in December 2000 and be replaced with an approach based on a combined market-share threshold of 20%.[38]

3.5. Technology Transfer

Commission Regulation No. 240/96 is designed to promote the transfer of technology by exempting qualified arrangements for the licensing of patents and know-how.[39] Under Article 8(1)(d), "patents" include topographies of semiconductor products as discussed at Chapter 6 Section 4 below. The Regulation also extends to agreements containing other intellectual property, such as copyrighted software, which contributes to the licensed technology and is only ancillary.[40] The basic exemption in Article 1 is for exclusivity and various forms of territorial protection for specified time periods. Articles 2 and 3 cover numerous other provisions including minimum quantities, field-of-use restrictions, and quality specifications. Patent pools, joint ventures, or reciprocal licenses are generally excluded unless they comply with the detailed requirements in Article 5. The Regulation remains in effect through March 2006.[41]

4. Merger Control Regulation

4.1. Community Dimension

Council Regulation No. 4064/89 establishes a system for prior notification and review of significant mergers with Community-wide impact to ensure that they do not impair effective competition within the common market.[42] Article 1(1) makes the Regulation applicable to all concentrations with a "Community dimension". Under Article 1(2), this is where the combined aggregate worldwide turnover of all the parties exceeds EUR 5

OJ No. L21/8 (January 29, 1993), and Commission Regulation No. 2236/97, OJ No. L306/12 (November 11, 1997).

37 See Articles 2 and 3 of Regulation No. 417/85 as amended.

38 Article 10 of Regulation No. 417/85 as amended. For the Commission proposal, see the citation at note 35 above.

39 Commission Regulation No. 240/96 on the application of Article 81(3) of the Treaty to certain categories of technology transfer agreements, OJ No. L31/2 (February 9, 1996). This consolidates and supersedes the prior block exemptions for patents and know-how in Commission Regulations No. 2349/84 and No. 556/89, respectively. See Article 11 and Recitals 2 and 3 of Regulation No. 240/96.

40 See Articles 1(1), 5(1)(4) and 10(15), and Recital 6 of Regulation No. 240/96. Article 5(1)(5) and Recital 8 make clear that the Regulation is not applicable to agreements solely for the purpose of sale including marketing know-how in the context of franchising.

41 Article 13 of Regulation No. 240/96.

42 Council Regulation No. 4064/89 on the control of concentrations between undertakings, OJ No. L257/13 (September 21, 1990), as amended by Council Regulation No. 1310/97, OJ No. L180/1 (July 9, 1997).

billion, and the aggregate Community-wide turnover of at least two exceeds EUR 250 million each, unless each of them derives more than two-thirds in the same Member State.[43]

For mergers not meeting those thresholds, Article 1(3) provides that a Community dimension also exists for worldwide and Community turnover of EUR 2.5 billion and EUR 100 million, respectively, as long as there are adequate levels of activity in each of at least three Member States.[44]

Subject to judicial review, the Commission has exclusive jurisdiction to enforce the Regulation, and Member States may not apply their national competition law to any concentration with a Community dimension.[45] In appropriate circumstances, the Commission may refer a case involving distinct local markets to national authorities, and may act at the request of one or more Member States if a concentration which lacks a Community dimension threatens competition within their territory.[46]

4.2. Concentrations and Joint Ventures

Under Article 3(1), a "concentration" arises where two or more independent firms merge, or one acquires direct or indirect control of all or part of another firm by purchase of securities or assets, contract, or any other means. Article 3(2) extends this to joint ventures which perform all the functions of an autonomous economic entity on a lasting basis (full-function joint ventures).[47]

Where a full-function joint venture has the object or effect of coordinating the competitive behavior of firms that remain independent, those aspects are evaluated under the Merger Control Regulation in accordance with the criteria in Articles 81(1) and (3) of the Treaty.[48] Other joint ventures remain subject to the procedures at Section 2.2 above.[49]

4.3. Substantive Evaluation

Articles 2(2) and (3) require concentrations to be declared compatible or incompatible with the common market based on whether they create or strengthen a dominant position

---

43 The rules for calculating turnover are in Article 5 of Regulation No. 4064/89 as amended. See also the Commission notices on the concept of "undertakings" and the calculation of turnover at OJ No. C66/14 and OJ No. C66/25 (March 2, 1998), respectively.

44 In each Member State, combined aggregate turnover for all parties of more than EUR 100 million, with the turnover of at least two of them exceeding EUR 25 million each.

45 Articles 21(1) and (2) of Regulation No. 4064/89 as amended. Under Article 21(3), Member States may take appropriate measures to protect their legitimate interests in other areas such as public security, prudential rules, and plurality of the media.

46 Articles 9 and 22(3), respectively, of Regulation No. 4064/89 as amended.

47 See the Commission notices on the concepts of "concentration" and "full-function joint ventures" at OJ No. C66/1 and OJ No. C66/5 (March 2, 1998).

48 Article 2(4) of Regulation No. 4064/89 as amended.

49 In practice, this is limited to those which lack a Community dimension or are not full-function. See Article 22(1) of Regulation No. 4064/89 as amended, as well as the Commission information on the assessment of full-function joint ventures under the competition rules, OJ No. C66/38 (March 2, 1998).

which would significantly impair competition in the Community or a substantial part of it. Under Article 2(1), the Commission is directed to take into account the structure of the markets and the actual or potential competition including the following specific factors:

- Market position of the parties and their economic and financial power.[50]
- Alternatives available to suppliers and users and their access to supplies or markets.
- Any legal or other barriers to entry.
- Supply and demand trends for the goods and services.
- Interests of intermediate and ultimate purchasers.
- Development of technical and economic progress provided that it benefits consumers and does not form an obstacle to competition.

In evaluating the coordination aspects of full-function joint ventures in accordance with Article 2(4), the Commission must also examine:

- Any significant activities retained by the parent companies in the same market as the joint venture or in upstream, downstream, or neighboring markets.
- The possibility of eliminating substantial competition in the relevant products or services as a result of the coordination which arises from creation of the joint venture.

4.4. Procedure

Under Article 4 of the Regulation, all concentrations with a Community dimension must be notified to the Commission within one week after entering an agreement, announcing a public bid, or acquiring a controlling interest. The detailed rules for notification and other procedures are prescribed by Commission Regulation No. 447/98.[51]

Upon examining the notification, the Commission may decide that the transaction does not fall within the scope of the Regulation, that there is no reason for opposition since it is compatible with the common market, or that proceedings should be initiated because there are serious doubts as to compatibility.[52] After initiation, the Commission may find the concentration compatible or incompatible with the common market.[53] Under Article 8(4), they may require divestiture, cessation of joint control, or other appropriate action to restore effective competition.

---

[50] There is a presumption of compatibility where the parties' share of the relevant market does not exceed 25%. See Recital 15 of Regulation No. 4064/89 as amended.

[51] Commission Regulation No. 447/98 on notifications, time limits, and hearings provided for in Council Regulation No. 4064/89 on the control of concentrations between undertakings, OJ No. L61/1 (March 2, 1998). The notification is submitted in accordance with Form CO which calls for information and supporting evidence on the parties, nature of the transaction, ownership and control, personal and financial links, product and geographic markets, other affected markets, turnover in relevant sectors, structures of supply and demand, research and development, barriers to entry, and any ancillary restraints.

[52] Article 6 of Regulation No. 4064/89 as amended. Under Articles 6(1)(b) and 8(2), a decision of compatibility also covers any ancillary restrictions which are directly related and necessary to implementation of the transaction.

[53] Articles 8(2) and (3) of Regulation No. 4064/89 as amended. A decision on compatibility may include conditions and obligations necessary to ensure that the parties comply with any commitments made to the Commission.

The Regulation establishes stringent time limits which generally oblige the Commission to determine whether to initiate proceedings within one month of notification, and to issue any ruling on incompatibility within four months thereafter.[54] Other important provisions cover suspensive effect, Commission powers to investigate and obtain information, and the potential imposition of substantial fines and periodic penalty payments for violations of the applicable requirements.[55]

For illustrative decisions by the Commission, see the summaries in the Appendix on:

- The horizontal, vertical and conglomerate aspects of a merger between computer and telecommunications manufacturers (*AT&T/NCR*, Section 6.3.1).
- Problems of market definition and analysis in dynamic growth industries such as the information services sector (*Digital/Philips* and *EDS/SD-Scicon*, Sections 6.3.2 and 6.3.3).
- Imposition of a fine for the failure to make timely notification and obtain prior approval for an acquisition in the manufacture and sale of personal computers (*Samsung/AST*, Section 6.3.4).
- Approval of a full-function joint venture for the provision of Internet gateway and related services in Sweden including the potential coordination of competitive behavior on the neighboring market for dial-up network access (*Schibsted Multimedia/Telenor/Telia*, Section 6.3.5).

5. State Aid

These rules appear in Articles 87 through 89 of the Treaty.[56]

Under Article 87(1), it is generally considered incompatible with the common market for Member States to use public resources in a manner which may distort competition and affect trade by favoring certain enterprises or the production of certain goods.[57] The Commission is charged with keeping this under review and requiring incompatible aid to be abolished or modified within a prescribed period.[58] To make this effective, Article 88(3) obliges the Member States to notify the Commission of any plans to grant or alter aid and to delay implementation pending examination and final decision.[59]

In accordance with Article 89, the Council may enact appropriate measures for the application of these provisions including the conditions for notification under Article 88(3). In doing so, they have authorized the Commission to issue block exemption

---

[54] Articles 10(1)–(3) of Regulation No. 4064/89 as amended. Under Article 10(6), the concentration shall be "deemed to have been declared compatible" if the Commission fails to comply with the prescribed time periods.

[55] Articles 7 and 11–16 of Regulation No. 4064/89 as amended.

[56] These were formerly Articles 92–94 before the changes in the Amsterdam Treaty.

[57] There are specified exceptions in Articles 87(2) and (3) including aid for social purposes, natural disasters, economic development of disadvantaged areas, cultural preservation, and other categories identified by the Council acting on a proposal from the Commission.

[58] Articles 88(1) and (2) of the Treaty. Article 88(2) provides for a direct reference to the Court of Justice in case of non-compliance with the Commission's decision.

[59] See Council Regulation No. 659/1999 laying down detailed rules for the application of Article 88 of the Treaty, OJ No. L83/1 (March 27, 1999).

regulations for certain categories of aid which are considered compatible with the common market and are therefore not required to be notified.[60]

For a representative decision in this area, see the Commission's ruling in *Groupe Bull* (Section 6.4.1) which approved the French Government's recapitalization program for an ailing diversified computer manufacturer as part of a restructuring plan aimed at restoring profitability and encouraging rapid privatization with a new industrial partner.

6. Appendix: Selected Cases

6.1. Article 81

6.1.1. Computerland[61]

This involved a standard distribution franchise agreement to employ Computerland's technical and commercial know-how for the sale of microcomputers from a wide range of different manufacturers to end-users in Europe. The Commission determined that Article 81(1) was not applicable to provisions which were necessary to prevent the franchisor's know-how from benefiting competitors and to maintain the identity and reputation of the sales network. However, there were prohibited restrictions from location and exclusivity clauses which resulted in a degree of market-sharing among the parties, along with the obligation to sell only to end-users or other Computerland franchisees since this limited their commercial freedom and deprived third-party resellers of sources of supply. The Commission nevertheless granted an individual exemption under Article 81(3) because the Computerland system improved distribution by promoting competition both within the network and with numerous rival outlets.[62] In addition, the franchisees were free to set their own prices, actively seek customers, and choose suppliers of approved products. The restrictions were considered indispensable since potential franchisees would not have made the necessary investment without some territorial protection, and the limitation to end-users was central to the concept of a retail network providing products and services to final consumers.

6.1.2. Fujitsu AMD Semiconductor[63]

The parties formed a joint venture to design, construct, and operate a plant in Japan for the production of a new generation of integrated circuits known as EPROMs and flash

---

[60] Council Regulation No. 994/98 on the application of Articles 87 and 88 of the Treaty to certain categories of horizontal state aid, OJ No. L142/1 (May 14, 1998). Under Articles 1(1) and 2(1), this covers regional and *de minimis* aid, as well as aid for small- and medium-sized enterprises, research and development, environmental protection, employment, and training. See also the Commission notice on Community guidelines on state aid for rescuing and restructuring firms in difficulty, OJ No. C288/2 (October 9, 1999).

[61] Case No. IV/32.034, OJ No. L222/12 (August 10, 1987). See also European Commission 17th Report on Competition Policy 1987 at ¶66.

[62] The Computerland arrangements went beyond the scope of the block exemptions for exclusive distribution and purchasing in Regulations No. 1983/83 and No. 1984/83, and the exemption for franchising agreements in Regulation No. 4087/88 was not yet enacted. See Section 3.1 and 3.2 above.

[63] Case No. IV/34.891, OJ No. L341/66 (December 30, 1994). See also Commission press-release IP(94)1203 (December 13, 1994) and the European Commission 24th Report on Competition Policy 1994 at ¶¶163–177 and Annex II page 347.

memories based on 0.5 micron technology. This included ancillary provisions for non-competition and prior approval for the assignment of intellectual property. In addition, there were related agreements for technology licensing, joint development, and reciprocal investments. The Commission found a violation of Article 81(1) from establishment of the joint venture since both parents were actual competitors on the relevant market. They also arranged for territorial limitations on their active sales within Europe which had the effect of partitioning the market (a similar allocation for Asia and the Americas was not considered restrictive because it did not impair European trade). An exemption was granted under Article 81(3) since these sophisticated devices would directly benefit consumers through higher-performance innovative products. The restrictions inherent in the joint venture were essential to sharing the considerable risks and costs of manufacturing complex items with short life-cycles. Territorial protection still permitted unsolicited orders, was for a relatively brief period (five years), and would promote customer acceptance of the new products since the respective areas reflected the parties' established infrastructure including networks for after-sales service.

6.1.3. Olivetti/Digital[64]

This strategic alliance was based on the licensing of Digital's Alpha AXP technology to Olivetti using a new RISC (reduced instruction set computer) microprocessor. For a renewable five-year term, Olivetti committed to Alpha AXP for all its computer platforms and related software except those with Intel microprocessors. Olivetti also had a four-year obligation to purchase products using Alpha AXP technology from Digital. Under the circumstances, the Commission concluded that there was no violation of Article 81(1) from the licensing agreement because Olivetti needed a full-line of RISC computers but lacked the resources to develop them on its own. The commitment to Digital therefore did not restrict Olivetti's competitive freedom beyond what was inherent in the selection of any specific RISC platform. On the other hand, the purchase requirement restricted Olivetti's ability to choose suppliers and eliminated that company as a potential customer for future licensees of Digital's Alpha AXP. An exemption was warranted since this promoted more rapid dissemination of the technology including the development of software designed for RISC architecture. Large-scale production by Digital could only be assured by an adequate purchasing commitment during the critical start-up phase. Any significant adverse effect on competition was unlikely because other firms were supplying their own versions of RISC computers.

6.1.4. STACK International[65]

The Commission issued an administrative comfort letter confirming that there was no restriction of competition from the activities of STACK International, a non-profit organization created and administered by major European, Japanese, and U.S. companies in the

---

64 Case No. IV/34.410, OJ No. L309/24 (December 2, 1994). See also European Commission 24th Report on Competition Policy 1994 at ¶¶161–162 and Annex II page 345.

65 Commission press-release IP(98)788 (September 3, 1998).

information technology sector. STACK defined generic specifications and standards for electronic components such as integrated circuits and memory modules, and certified compliance by products and manufacturers. It also monitored prices paid by member companies and reported on the resulting benchmarks. Membership was not exclusive and did not restrict the competitive freedom of the parties in the purchase or sale of the relevant items. There was no exchange of commercially-sensitive information since this only involved basic components. Individual prices were kept strictly confidential with benchmarks limited to products reported by at least three firms.

6.1.5. Systemform[66]

This was a German company which manufactured machinery for handling and processing large computer printouts. The case arose on a complaint from the French distributor Novalliance. After investigation, the Commission determined that Systemform's exclusive agreements with national distributors violated Article 81(1) by prohibiting sales outside their contract territories as well as to customers within those territories with the known intention to export. The agreements also required resale prices to be set jointly by Systemform and its distributors or that Systemform be kept advised of pricing and discounts. These restrictions went beyond the scope of the block exemption for exclusive distribution in Commission Regulation No. 1983/83. They did not qualify for individual exemption since there was no notification and the proscribed clauses failed to comply with Article 81(3). In evaluating the appropriate sanction, the Commission considered the gravity and duration of the infringement including the clear violations from the territorial and pricing restrictions which reflected a consistent policy over a long period. On the other hand, Systemform did not dispute these findings, there was no clear effort by the company to enforce the illegal provisions, and they had already taken steps to bring their distribution arrangements into conformity with Community law. The Commission imposed a fine in the amount of EUR 100,000.

6.1.6. X/Open Group[67]

In order to increase the adaptability of their products, a group of large computer manufacturers agreed to develop standard interface definitions for applications software to be used with the Unix operating system. The resulting definitions were publicly available and constituted an open industry standard. However, the Commission found a restriction of competition from the critical lead-time gained by members of the group coupled with their discretionary power to exclude new applicants for membership. An exemption was granted in view of the clear benefits from establishing a common applications environment for Unix. Because the information was published promptly, third parties were able to produce

[66] Case No. IV/35.679, OJ No. L47/11 (February 18, 1997). See also Commission press-release IP(96)1124 (December 4, 1996) and the European Commission 26th Competition Report 1996 at ¶52 and Part Two page 119.

[67] Case No. IV/31.458, OJ No. L35/36 (February 6, 1987). See also European Commission 16th Report on Competition Policy 1986 at ¶65.

compatible items with minimal delay. The membership procedures were necessary to guarantee adequate commitment and enhance efficiency by keeping the group to a manageable size. To ensure that the criteria were applied in a reasonable manner, the Commission required annual reports on any rejected applicants or changes in membership.

6.2. Article 82

6.2.1. Digital Equipment[68]

The Commission accused Digital of abusing a dominant position in the markets for hardware and software services for Digital computers through exclusionary practices aimed at third-party maintenance companies. The specific charges involved discriminatory pricing for software and tying the supply of hardware and software maintenance by offering the latter at a considerably lower price as part of a "DSS package" than when offered alone. Other contracts provided fidelity discounts conditional on users not dealing with third parties. Digital contested these allegations but agreed to modify its policies by offering hardware maintenance on a stand-alone basis and pricing software with a simple flat fee. Prices for the DSS package would not be less than 90% of the sum of the individual items, with price lists to be made public including separate quotes for each component. Discounts and allowances must be transparent and non-discriminatory, above average total cost, and equivalent for DSS and individual services. Finally, Digital's authorized distributors were required to be selected in accordance with objective criteria to avoid excluding third-party maintenance providers. The Digital undertaking runs from October 1997 until January 2003 with a right of review in the year 2000. Existing long-term contracts could be terminated at the user's option from October 1998.

6.2.2. IBM[69]

In December 1980, the Commission opened proceedings against IBM for abusing a dominant position in their System 370 computers by withholding critical interface information, memory and software bundling, and refusing to supply certain software to users of non-IBM central processing units (CPUs). The company denied the allegations but subsequently revised its practices for the supply and bundling of software. The remaining claims were resolved in a formal undertaking accepted by the Commission in August 1984. Under the terms, IBM agreed to offer its System 370 CPUs either without main memory or with only such capacity as strictly necessary for testing. They were also required to make timely disclosure of sufficient interface information to enable competitors to attach their hardware and software products including interconnection via Systems Network Architecture. The duration of the undertaking was indefinite with IBM having the right to give notice of termination from January 1990. After appropriate notice, this ended in July 1995.[70]

---

68 Commission press-relese IP(97)868 (October 10, 1997). See also European Commission 27th Report on Competition Policy 1997 at ¶69 and Part Two page 153.

69 European Commission 14th Report on Competition Policy 1984 at ¶¶94–95.

70 European Commission 24th Report on Competition Policy 1994 at Annex II page 365.

6.2.3. Microsoft[71]

This case was initiated on a complaint from Novell concerning anticompetitive practices by Microsoft in the market for operating systems software for personal computers. The Commission's investigation focused on per-processor and per-system licenses which required manufacturers to pay royalties regardless whether their computers were shipped with pre-installed Microsoft software, along with commitments to a fixed minimum quantity of a particular product regardless of actual use. After detailed negotiations, Microsoft agreed to delete the per-processor and minimum quantity requirements and to limit the duration of licenses to one year. Per-system obligations were only permitted if licensees had the option to obtain non-Microsoft products without payment of royalties. Offending provisions in existing contracts were not to be enforced and licensees could terminate at their discretion. The undertaking was signed in July 1994 for a period of 6½ years. Similar allegations in the U.S. were resolved by a consent decree between Microsoft and the U.S. Department of Justice.

6.3. Merger Control Regulation

6.3.1. AT&T/NCR[72]

This was an unsolicited cash tender offer by AT&T to acquire NCR as a wholly-owned subsidiary. The Commission cleared the transaction under Article 6(1)(b) of the Regulation after examining the horizontal, vertical, and conglomerate aspects of the merger. For personal and small multiuser computers, the parties' combined market-share below 10% did not create or strengthen a dominant position. In calculating this figure, the Commission excluded AT&T's shareholding of 20% or less in Olivetti which did not confer "decisive influence" within the meaning of the Regulation. The vertical synergies from linking AT&T's Unix operating software with NCR's leading position in financial and retail workstations were unlikely to disadvantage competitors in view of AT&T's licensing policies and the movement toward open systems. Finally, any conglomerate effects involving NCR workstations and AT&T's networking know-how were speculative and would be counterbalanced by other major international companies active in both the computer and telecommunications sectors.

6.3.2. Digital/Philips[73]

The Commission approved the acquisition by Digital of Philips' information services activities. There were separate product markets for small- and medium-sized multiuser computers, financial workstations, software, and hardware maintenance. The highest share of approximately 22% was in financial workstations where Digital was one of the

---

[71] Commission press-release IP(94)653 (July 17, 1994). See also European Commission 24th Report on Competition Policy 1994 at ¶¶193–212 and Annex II page 364. For a summary of this and other investigations involving Microsoft, see Commission press-release IP(00)141 (February 10, 2000).

[72] Case No. IV/M.050 (January 18, 1991), 1992 CMLR M41. See also European Commission 21st Report on Competition Policy 1991 at Annex III page 369.

[73] Case No. IV/M.129 (September 2, 1991), 1994-4 CMLR M4.

three leading firms. However, the Commission specifically noted that large shares of dynamic growth industries are not extraordinary and may not reflect market power particularly if there are regular changes in leadership. Ancillary provisions for non-competition and the supply of components were considered directly related and necessary to implementation of the merger.

6.3.3. EDS/SD-Scicon[74]

This sheds additional light on the Commission's approach to market definition in the information services sector. They began by underscoring the inherent analytical difficulties since the various categories are often blurred.[75] One possible method was to focus on the market segments for systems management and operations, systems integration, pure consulting, and processing services. Alternatively, it could be based on clients served in areas such as banking and finance, discrete manufacturing, and process manufacturing. Finally, they might look at the industry purchasing the services. In this situation, the Commission was able to approve the merger without making a definitive judgment in view of the fragmented markets, low entry barriers, high degree of supply and demand substitutability, and parties' low combined share which never exceeded 13% by any relevant standard.

6.3.4. Samsung/AST[76]

The Commission imposed a fine of EUR 33,000 on the Korean company Samsung for failing to make timely notification and obtain prior approval for the acquisition of AST in the manufacture and sale of personal computers. Samsung took control of AST in January 1996 but did not notify the transaction until April 1997 in violation of Articles 4(1) and 7(1) of the Regulation. In determining the amount of the fine in accordance with Article 14, the Commission considered the gravity and duration of the infringement as well as a number of aggravating and mitigating factors. On the positive side, there was no damaging effect on competition, the default appeared unintentional, and Samsung eventually notified the operation and cooperated with the Commission in the investigation. On the other hand, the infringement lasted for a considerable period and Samsung should have known better as a major international firm with significant activities in Europe. This was the first decision by the Commission under Article 14 of the Regulation.

6.3.5. Schibsted Multimedia/Telenor/Telia[77]

The Commission approved this full-function joint venture for the provision of Internet gateway and related services in Sweden. In evaluating the competitive effects, they identified

---

[74] Case No. IV/M.112 (July 17, 1991), 1993–4 CMLR M77.

[75] Compare the Commission statement at Section 2.1 above on the complexity of market definition in high-technology sectors.

[76] Case No.IV/M.920, OJ No. L225/12 (August 26, 1999). The decision approving the underlying transaction is reported at OJ No. C203/3 (July 3, 1997). See also Commission press-releases IP(97)505 (June 10, 1997) and IP(98)166 (February 18, 1998).

[77] Case No. IV/JV.1 (May 27, 1998), 1999-4 CMLR 216. See also Commission press-release IP(98)476 (May 28, 1998).

separate markets for Internet advertising, paid-for content, and website production. In each case, there was no question of dominance since the segments were growing rapidly and the parents had maximum individual shares of 10–20% and usually much lower. Under Article 2(4) of the Regulation, the Commission was also required to examine the potential coordination of competitive behavior between the parties, including closely neighboring markets, in accordance with the criteria in Article 81 of the Treaty. There were no such aspects for Internet advertising and paid-for content, and coordination on website production would not be appreciable in view of the relevant shares of 5% or less. Finally, they analyzed the adjoining market for dial-up Internet access where two of the parents had substantial shares between 25–40% and 10–25%, respectively. Any appreciable restriction was considered unlikely because of the high growth, low entry barriers, and price sensitivity of the market and its relatively large size in comparison with that of the joint venture.

6.4. State Aid

6.4.1. Groupe Bull[78]

This involved a French manufacturer of diversified computer products including software and maintenance services. The majority share capital was held by the French Government either directly or through France Telecom. There were minority shareholdings by the private companies IBM and NEC. The French Government undertook a program to recapitalize Bull in the total amount of FF 11.1 billion comprising an advance of FF 2.5 billion and a further increase of FF 8.6 billion.

In evaluating whether this constituted aid within the meaning of Article 87(1) of the Treaty, the Commission reviewed the situation in accordance with the "market economy investor principle" as of the time the decisions to increase capital were made in February 1993 and December 1993, respectively. During the relevant period, Bull's financial position was weak, there was no prospect of an adequate return within a reasonable period, and the company would not have been able to raise similar amounts in the capital markets on its own. A net present-value analysis confirmed that private investors would be unlikely to participate in such a transaction under normal conditions, and in fact Bull's two minority shareholders did not: IBM made no contribution at all and NEC's additional investment of FF 379 million, while proportional to its 4.4% interest, was not economically significant in comparison to the total amounts committed and that company's financial assets. The Commission therefore determined this to be aid but permitted it to go forward under Article 87(3)(c) which provides a derogation to facilitate economic development as long as there is no effect on trading conditions to an extent contrary to the common interest.

[78] Commission Decision No. 94/1073 concerning the grant of state aid by France to Groupe Bull in the form of a non-notified capital increase, OJ No. L386/1 (December 31, 1994). By Decision No. 94/220, OJ No. L107/61 (April 28, 1994), the Commission previously required France to suspend payments to Groupe Bull in violation of the standstill obligation in Article 88(3) of the Treaty. See also European Commission 24th Report on Competition Policy 1994 at Annex II page 493 and European Commission 23rd Report on Competition Policy 1993 at ¶400.

In arriving at this decision, the Commission underscored the desirability of establishing a viable and competitive information-technology industry provided that other European firms were not unduly disadvantaged. On the issue of viability, the aid was linked to a detailed restructuring plan which projected sound financial results for Bull within two years and would set the stage for rapid privatization with a new industrial partner. Adverse effects on other companies would be minimal since the restructuring involved significant capacity reductions and did not exceed what was strictly necessary. The Commission's approval was conditional on implementation of the plan within the agreed timetable, regular progress reports, and no further aid except in conformity with legal requirements including guidelines applicable to the carry-forward of any losses.

CHAPTER 6

INTELLECTUAL PROPERTY

A dynamic information technology sector requires the effective protection and enforcement of intellectual property rights in order to encourage innovation and widespread distribution of the resulting benefits.[1] At present, this remains largely a matter for the individual Member States.[2] However, certain rules have developed at Community level which play an important role in harmonizing national law.[3] The sections below describe the general regulatory framework for intellectual property along with the detailed provisions which apply to the legal protection of computer software, databases, and semiconductor topographies.

1. General

1.1. Copyright

The Commission is well aware of the significance of copyright to their information society initiatives.[4] To date, Community legislation has focused on harmonizing the term of protection coupled with the application of copyright to selected areas including satellite broadcasting, cable retransmission, and rental and lending activities.[5] In addition, there is

---

1 See Section 1 of Chapter 3 above which identifies this as a necessary element to create a favorable business environment for the information society. This is reinforced by the competition law aspects of intellectual property licensing covered at Sections 2.2, 3.3, and 3.5 of Chapter 5.

2 Article 295 of the Treaty (former Article 222) expressly indicates that it shall in no way prejudice the rules of the Member States on property ownership. See also Article 30 (former Article 36) which makes an exception to the prohibition against quantitative restrictions for national measures protecting industrial and commercial property.

3 These rules are consistent with the WTO agreement on trade-related aspects of intellectual property rights (TRIPs) at Section 1.1 of Chapter 4 above. The complete text of the WTO TRIPs agreement is published at OJ No. L336/213 (December 23, 1994). Specific provisions will be referenced as appropriate. See also Section 4.4 of Chapter 4 on Council Regulation No. 3295/94 which prohibits unlawful trade in products which infringe certain intellectual property rights including counterfeit or pirated goods.

4 See the Commission communication concerning the Green Paper on copyright and related rights in the information society, COM(96)568 (November 20, 1996); Commission Green Paper on copyright and related rights in the information society, COM(95)382 (July 19, 1995); and Commission Green Paper on copyright and the challenge of technology – issues requiring immediate action, COM(88)172 (June 7, 1988).

5 Council Directive No. 93/98 harmonizing the term of protection of copyright and certain related rights, OJ No. L290/9 (November 24, 1993); Council Directive No. 93/83 on the coordination of certain rules concerning copyright and related rights applicable to satellite broadcasting and cable re-transmission, OJ No. L248/15 (October 6, 1993); and Council Directive No. 92/100 on rental and lending rights and certain rights related to copyright in the field of intellectual property, OJ No. L346/61 (November 27, 1992). These

a pending proposal which would extend coverage to digital interactive services and equipment both on-line and incorporated in physical media such as compact disks, CD-ROMs, and digital video disks.[6]

1.2. Industrial Design

Directive No. 98/71 protects industrial designs by a system of registration which confers exclusive rights on the holder.[7] Under Article 1(b), the definition of "product" excludes computer programs. To qualify, Article 3(2) requires a design to be new and have an individual character. The term is for renewable periods of five years up to a maximum of 25 years from the date of filing.[8] Items remain eligible for copyright and other forms of protection including unregistered designs, patents, trademarks, and utility models.[9] An accompanying proposal for a Regulation would be fully compatible with Directive No. 98/71 and create a unitary right valid throughout the Community based on a single registration with the Office for Harmonization in the Internal Market located in Alicante, Spain.[10]

1.3. Patents and Utility Models

There is a method for obtaining patents under the national laws of the individual Member States by applying to the European Patent Office in Munich.[11] However, none of the efforts to establish a genuine Community-wide patent has yet been ratified.[12] The Commission considers this unsatisfactory and is proposing a new Community patent which would co-exist with those issued by the Member States and the European Patent Office.[13] This would be accompanied by measures for the harmonization of national law

measures include references to the Computer Software Directive discussed in greater detail at Section 2 below. See also Articles 9–14 of the WTO TRIPs agreement cited at note 3 above, as well as Council Decision No. 2000/278 approving the WIPO Copyright Treaty and WIPO Performances and Phonograms Treaty on behalf of the European Community, OJ No. L89/6 (April 11, 2000).

6 Commission proposal for a European Parliament and Council Directive on the harmonization of certain aspects of copyright and related rights in the information society, OJ No. C108/6 (April 7, 1998), as amended at OJ No. C180/6 (June 25, 1999). See also Commission press-releases IP(97)1100 (December 10, 1997) and IP(99)337 (May 21, 1999).

7 Article 3(1) of Directive No. 98/71 of the European Parliament and Council on the legal protection of designs, OJ No. L289/28 (October 28, 1998). Under Article 19, Member States are required to implement the Directive by October 2001. See also Articles 25 and 26 of the WTO TRIPs agreement at note 3 above.

8 Article 10 of Directive No. 98/71.

9 Articles 16 and 17 of Directive No. 98/71.

10 See Commission press-release IP(99) 407 (June 22, 1999). The latest version of the proposal is not yet published in the Official Journal.

11 Munich convention on the grant of European patents (October 5, 1973).

12 See the convention for the European patent for the common market, OJ No. L17/1 (January 26, 1976), as amended by the Luxembourg agreement relating to Community patents, OJ No. L401/1 (December 30, 1989).

13 See Commission press-releases IP(99)105 (February 12, 1999) and IP(97)558 (June 25, 1997), along with the Commission Green Paper on the Community patent and the patent system in Europe: promoting innovation through patents, COM(97)314 (June 24, 1997). See also Articles 27–34 of the WTO TRIPs agreement at note 3 above.

to extend protection to computer software and provide for eventual accession by the EU to the Munich arrangements.

Utility models are registered rights for technical inventions which are more flexible and less expensive than patents.[14] There is a proposal here as well which in the current version would not cover presentations of information or inventions involving computer programs.[15]

1.4. Trademarks

Legislation in this area comprises both approximation of national law and a Community-wide trademark issued by the Office for Harmonization in the Internal Market.[16] Provisions for the Community trademark prescribe detailed rules for applications, registration, duration and renewal, surrender, revocation, invalidity, collective marks, and other procedural matters. The Commission has enacted further implementing measures including specific subjects such as fees payable and administrative appeals.[17]

2. Computer Software

Council Directive No. 91/250 establishes the basic rules for the legal protection of computer software as intellectual property in the Community.[18] The purpose is to safeguard the substantial investment of human, technical, and financial resources necessary to develop a computer program by prohibiting misappropriation through unauthorized reproduction, imitation, or counterfeiting.[19] The detailed provisions are summarized below.

---

[14] See Commission press-release IP(97)1127 (December 16, 1997) and Commission Green Paper on protection of utility models in the single market, COM(95)370 (July 19, 1995).

[15] See Articles 3(2)(d) and 4(d) of the Commission proposal for a European Parliament and Council Directive approximating the legal arrangements for the protection of inventions by utility model, OJ No. C36/13 (February 3, 1998). Suggested amendments by the European Parliament appear at OJ No. C175/424 (June 21, 1999).

[16] Council Directive No. 89/104 approximating the laws of the Member States relating to trademarks, OJ No. L40/1 (February 11, 1989), and Council Regulation No. 40/94 on the Community trademark, OJ No. L11/1 (January 14, 1994), as amended by Council Regulation No. 3288/94, OJ No. L349/83 (December 31, 1994). See also Articles 15–21 of the WTO TRIPs agreement at note 3 above.

[17] Commission Regulation No. 2868/95 implementing Council Regulation No. 40/94 on the Community trademark, OJ No. L303/1 (December 15, 1995); Commission Regulation No. 2869/95 on the fees payable to the Office for Harmonization in the Internal Market, OJ No. L303/33 (December 15, 1995); and Commission Regulation No. 216/96 laying down rules of procedure for the Boards of Appeal of the Office for Harmonization in the Internal Market, OJ No. L28/11 (February 6, 1996).

[18] Council Directive No. 91/250 on the legal protection of computer programs, OJ No. L122/42 (May 17, 1991). Under Article 10(1) of the Directive, Member States were required to enact appropriate implementing legislation before January 1993. For further background, see the Commission's original proposal including explanatory memorandum at OJ No. C91/4 (April 12, 1989) and the amended version at OJ No. C320/22 (December 20, 1990).

[19] See Recital 2 of Directive No. 91/250 and ¶1.3 (Part one) of the Commission explanatory memorandum at note 18 above.

2.1. Scope and Limitations

Article 1(1) of the Directive requires Member States to protect computer programs as literary works within the meaning of the Berne Convention.[20] This covers the expression of a program in any form, along with preparatory design material, but does not apply to the ideas and principles underlying the elements of the software including those relating to interfaces.[21] In other respects, the definition is deliberately imprecise in order to avoid becoming outdated.[22]

Under Article 1(3), a program qualifies for protection if it is original in the sense of being the author's own intellectual creation. No other criteria are permitted.

2.2. Authors and Beneficiaries

The author of a program is the natural person or group who creates it, the legal entity designated by Member State legislation, or the person considered to be the author of a collective work.[23] Software created by employees within the scope of their duties belongs to the employer unless otherwise provided by contract.[24] Beneficiaries are all natural or legal persons eligible for protection under national copyright law as applied to literary works.[25]

2.3. Restricted Acts and Exceptions

In accordance with Articles 4(a) and (b), the rightholder is exclusively entitled to perform or authorize:

- Permanent or temporary reproduction of a program by any means and in any form, whether in whole or part, including loading, displaying, running, transmission, or storage.
- Translation, adaptation, arrangement, and any other alteration of a program and reproduction of the results, but without prejudice to the rights of the person making the alteration.

Absent specific contractual provisions, the foregoing acts do not require authorization where they are necessary for the lawful acquirer to use the program for the intended purpose which includes correction of errors.[26]

Under Article 4(c), the rightholder controls any form of distribution to the public such as sale or rental.[27] This is subject to the rule that the first sale in the Community of a copy

---

[20] This is consistent with Article 10(1) of the WTO TRIPs agreement, cited at note 3 above, which applies to computer programs whether in source or object code.

[21] Articles 1(1) and (2) and Recitals 7 and 13 of Directive No. 91/250. See also Recital 14 which indicates that logic, algorithms, and programming language are unprotected to the extent that they comprise ideas and principles.

[22] See ¶1.1 (Parts one and two) of the Commission explanatory memorandum at note 18 above.

[23] Article 2(1) of Directive No. 91/250. Article 2(2) specifies that rights are owned jointly where a group of natural persons creates a program jointly.

[24] Article 2(3) of Directive No. 91/250.

[25] Article 3 of Directive No. 91/250.

[26] Article 5(1) of Directive No. 91/250.

[27] Recital 16 of Directive No. 91/250 defines "rental" as making a program available for a limited period and for profit. Public lending for non-commercial purposes is outside the scope of the Directive. See also Article 11

of the program by the rightholder or with his consent "exhausts" the distribution right for that copy except for the control of further rental.[28]

Finally, Articles 5(2) and (3) enable a person with the right to use a computer program to:

- Make back-up copies insofar as necessary for that use.
- Observe, study, or test the functioning of the program in order to determine the ideas and principles underlying it while performing any of the acts of loading, displaying, running, transmitting, or storing which he is entitled to do.

Any contractual provisions to the contrary are null and void.[29]

2.4. *Decompilation*

Article 6 on decompilation or reverse-engineering is intended to promote the interoperability of computer software by making essential information available on access protocols and interfaces.[30] Under Article 6(1), authorization is not required where reproduction of the code and translation of its form are indispensable for this purpose provided that:

- The acts are performed on behalf of a person having the right to use a copy of the program and are confined to the parts necessary to achieve interoperability with another program.
- The necessary information has not previously been readily available to the authorized person.

Under Article 6(2), the information may not be used or given to others except as necessary for interoperability, or employed to develop, produce, or market a substantially similar program, or in any other manner which infringes copyright. This is reinforced by the prohibition in Article 6(3) against decompilation which prejudices the legitimate interests of the rightholder or conflicts with normal exploitation of the software.

2.5. *Special Remedies*

In addition to the general obligation to enforce the Directive, Article 7(1) requires Member States to enact appropriate remedies against persons who put into circulation or

---

of the WTO TRIPs agreement at note 3 above as well as Council Directive No. 92/100 on rental and lending rights at note 5. Article 3 of Directive No. 92/100 makes that legislation without prejudice to Article 4(c) of Directive No. 91/250. Under Article 5(2) of Directive No. 92/100, Member States which do not apply the exclusive public lending right to computer programs are nevertheless required to introduce a remuneration for authors.

28 The "exhaustion" doctrine was initially developed by the Court of Justice as applied to copyright in *Deutsche Grammophon v. Metro*, Case No. 78/70, 1971 ECR 487, 1971 CMLR 631. It has since been extended throughout the field of intellectual property. For a recent decision involving trademarks, see *Sebago v. G-B Unic,* Case No. C-173/98, OJ No. C246/7 (August 28, 1999).

29 Article 9(1) and Recital 26 of Directive No. 91/250.

30 See Recitals 21–24 of Directive No. 91/250 and ¶3.10–¶3.15 (Part one) of the Commission explanatory memorandum at note 18 above. Here, too, Article 9(1) and Recital 26 make any contractual provisions to the contrary null and void.

possess for commercial purposes:

- A copy of a computer program knowing or with reason to know that it is an infringing copy.
- Any means whose sole purpose is to facilitate the unauthorized removal or circumvention of any technical device which may have been applied to protect a program.

Under Article 7(2), an infringing copy of a program shall be liable to seizure. Article 7(3) enables Member States to apply the same remedy to any means for unauthorized circumvention or removal of a protective technical device.

2.6. *Term of Protection*

Article 8 of the Directive established a provisional term of protection which was superseded by Council Directive No. 93/98.[31] Under Article 1(1) of Directive No. 93/98, the basic term of protection for literary works within the meaning of the Berne Convention runs for the life of the author and for 70 years after death.

2.7. *Other Provisions*

The Directive is without prejudice to:

- Other legal provisions such as those for patents, trademarks, unfair competition, trade secrets, protection of semiconductor products, or contract.[32]
- The competition rules in Articles 81 and 82 of the Treaty if a dominant supplier refuses to make information available which is necessary for interoperability, and measures relating to interfaces or standardization in the information technology and telecommunications sectors.[33]

3. Databases

Databases are covered by Directive No. 96/9.[34] As with computer software, the purpose is to afford an appropriate and uniform level of protection to the makers in order to ensure

---

31 See Article 11(1) and Recital 15 of Directive No. 93/98 at note 5 above.

32 Article 9(1) of Directive No. 91/250. See Section 1.3 above on the Commission proposals to harmonize Member State patent law including the extension of patentability to software. As noted at Sections 1.2 and 1.3, Article 1(b) of Directive No. 98/71 on industrial designs and Article 4(d) of the proposal for a Directive on utility models both expressly exclude computer programs. The legal protection of semiconductor topographies is covered at Section 4 below.

33 Recitals 27 and 28 of Directive No. 91/250. See generally the discussion of the relationship between computer software and competition policy at Sections 2.1, 3.1, and 3.5 of Chapter 5 above.

34 Directive No. 96/9 of the European Parliament and Council on the legal protection of databases, OJ No. L77/20 (March 27, 1996). This is consistent with Article 10(2) of the WTO TRIPs agreement, cited at note 3 above, which extends copyright protection to compilations of data or other material whether in machine-readable or other form. Under Article 16(1) of the Directive, Member States were required to enact

adequate remuneration and safeguard their investments against unauthorized access and misappropriation.[35] Unlike software, however, the approach involves both copyright and a special or "sui generis" right as discussed below.

3.1. Scope and Limitations

Under Article 1(1), the Directive relates to the legal protection of databases in any form. Article 1(2) defines "database" as a collection of independent works, data, or other material arranged in a systematic or methodical way and individually accessible by electronic or other means. There is no requirement for materials to have been physically stored in an organized manner.[36] Access may be electronic or otherwise including electromagnetic, electro-optical, and analogous processes as well as devices such as CD-ROM and CD-i.[37]

Authors may decide whether and how to incorporate their works in a database and whether authorization should be exclusive.[38] The Directive applies to collections of artistic, literary, or musical items along with text, sound, images, numbers, facts, and data, but not to recordings or audiovisual, cinematographic, literary, or musical works as such.[39] Compilations of music on a compact disk are generally outside the scope of the Directive since they do not meet the requirements for protection.[40]

In addition to the collections themselves, coverage extends to material necessary for the operation or consultation of databases such as thesaurus or indexation systems.[41] However, this does not apply to computer programs used in making or operating a database accessible electronically which remain subject to Directive No. 91/250 at Section 2 above.[42]

3.2. Copyright

Article 3(1) of the Directive establishes copyright protection for databases which constitute the author's own intellectual creation by reason of the selection or arrangement of their contents. Originality is the sole criterion for eligibility.[43] Protection covers the structure of the database but not the contents and is without prejudice to any rights in the contents themselves.[44]

---

implementing legislation before January 1998. See also Article 14 and Recital 60 which contain transitional provisions for databases created and rights acquired before the effective date of the Directive.

35 See Recitals 6, 7, 12, 38–40, and 48 of Directive No. 96/9.

36 Recital 21 of Directive No. 96/9.

37 Recitals 13, 14, and 22 of Directive No. 96/9.

38 Recital 18 of Directive No. 96/9.

39 Recital 17 of Directive No. 96/9.

40 Recital 19 of Directive No. 96/9.

41 Recital 20 of Directive No. 96/9.

42 See Articles 1(3), 2(a), and Recital 23 of Directive No. 96/9.

43 Article 3(1) and Recital 16 of Directive No. 96/9.

44 Article 3(2) and Recitals 15, 26, and 27 of Directive No. 96/9. Recital 28 indicates that moral rights are outside the scope of the Directive.

Under Article 4(1), the author is the natural person or group who creates the database or the legal person designated as the rightholder by Member State legislation.[45] The author of the database has the exclusive right to perform or authorize:

- Temporary or permanent reproduction by any means, in any form, in whole or part.[46]
- Translation, adaptation, arrangement, or other alteration.[47]
- Any form of public distribution of the database or a copy, except that the first sale in the Community by the rightholder or with his consent exhausts the right to control resale of that copy within the Community.[48]
- Any communication, display, or performance to the public.[49]

Authorization is not required where performance of the foregoing acts is necessary for access and normal use of the database by the lawful user.[50] Under Article 6(2), Member States also have the option of limiting the exclusive rights of the author in cases involving:

- Reproduction of a non-electronic database for private purposes.
- Teaching or scientific research as long as the source is indicated and to the extent justified by a non-commercial purpose.
- Public security or an administrative or judicial proceeding.
- Other exceptions to copyright which are traditionally recognized under national law.

Any such limitations may not be applied in a manner which unreasonably prejudices the author's legitimate interests or conflicts with normal exploitation of the database.[51]

Finally, the rules for copyright on the rental, lending, and term of protection for databases are prescribed by Directives No. 92/100 and No. 93/98, respectively.[52]

3.3. Sui Generis Right

In addition to copyright, Article 7(1) of the Directive creates a "sui generis" or special right which enables the maker with a substantial investment in a database to prevent the extraction or re-utilization of all or a substantial part of its contents.[53]

---

45 Articles 4(2) and (3) cover collective works recognized by national law and joint ownership for databases created jointly by a group of natural persons. Under Recital 29, employers may be given the rights to databases made by employees within the scope of their duties absent contractual provisions to the contrary.

46 Article 5(a) of Directive No. 96/9.

47 Article 5(b) of Directive No. 96/9. In accordance with Article 5(e), this also applies to reproduction, distribution, communication, display, or performance to the public resulting from the acts in Article 5(b).

48 See article 5(c) and Recitals 30 and 31 of Directive No. 96/9, as well as Section 2.3 and note 28 above on the "exhaustion" doctrine. Under Recital 33, it should be noted that exhaustion does not apply to on-line databases or material copies made from them since these are considered to be services instead of goods. Unlike CD-ROM or CD-i where intellectual property is incorporated in a physical medium, every on-line service is an act which may be subject to authorization by the rightholder.

49 Article 5(d) of Directive No. 96/9.

50 Article 6(1) and Recital 34 of Directive No. 96/9. Under Article 15, any contractual provision to the contrary is null and void.

51 Article 6(3) and Recital 37 of Directive No. 96/9.

52 Articles 2(b) and (c) and Recitals 24 and 25 of Directive No. 96/9. See also Section 2.6 and note 5 above.

53 Recital 41 of Directive No. 96/9 considers the maker to be the person who takes the risk of investment and therefore excludes sub-contractors. Under Recital 42, the protection is against acts by any user which go

Under Article 7(2)(a), "extraction" is the permanent or temporary transfer of all or a substantial part of the contents to another medium by any means or in any form.[54] Article 7(2)(b) defines "re-utilization" as making all or a substantial part of the contents available to the public by distributing copies, renting, or on-line or other forms of transmission.[55] Public lending is not an act of extraction or re-utilization.[56]

The special right may be transferred, assigned, or licensed.[57] It applies regardless of the eligibility of the database or its contents for protection by copyright or otherwise and is without prejudice to any rights existing in those contents.[58]

For databases made available to the public, a lawful user may not be prevented from extracting or re-utilizing insubstantial parts of the contents except for acts which conflict with normal exploitation, unreasonably prejudice the legitimate interests of the maker, or prejudice the holder of the copyright or related right of the items contained in the database.[59] As with copyright at Section 3.2 above, Member States may also permit lawful users to access substantial parts of the contents without authorization in cases involving:[60]

- Extraction from non-electronic databases for private purposes.
- Teaching and scientific research provided that the source is identified and to the extent justified by the non-commercial purpose.
- Public security or administrative and judicial proceedings.

The term of protection for the special right is 15 years from completion of the database, and this may be extended another 15 years from whenever the database is first made available to the public before expiration of the original period.[61] A significant new investment qualifies the resulting database for its own term of protection.[62]

To be eligible for protection, the maker or rightholder must be a national of a Member State, have their habitual residence in the Community, or be a company formed under the

beyond his legitimate rights and cause significant harm to the investment. Article 7(5) also protects against repeated and systematic extraction or re-utilization of insubstantial parts of the contents of a database by acts which conflict with normal exploitation or unreasonably prejudice the legitimate interests of the maker. In connection with the special right, the term "substantial" is to be evaluated throughout the Directive both quantitatively and qualitatively. See, for example, Articles 7(1), 8(1), and 10(3).

54 See also Recital 44 which confirms that this includes transfers necessitated by on-screen display of the contents.

55 This is subject to the normal rule on exhaustion except for on-line transmission or any material copy made from it. See Recital 43 of Directive No. 96/9 and note 48 above.

56 Article 7(2) of Directive No. 96/9.

57 Article 7(3) of Directive No. 96/9.

58 Article 7(4) and Recitals 18, 45, and 46 of Directive No. 96/9.

59 Articles 8(1)–(3) and Recital 49 of Directive No. 96/9. Under Article 15, any contractual provisions to the contrary are null and void.

60 Articles 9(a)–(c) of Directive No. 96/9. Recital 50 confirms that these exceptions must not prejudice the exclusive rights of the maker to exploit the database and the purpose must not be commercial. See also Recital 52 which enables Member States with rules comparable to the special right to retain other traditional exceptions.

61 Articles 10(1) and (2) of Directive No. 96/9. Under Recital 53, the maker of the database has the burden of establishing the date of completion.

62 Article 10(3) and Recital 55 of Directive No. 96/9. The requisite change may include the accumulation of successive additions, deletions, or alterations as well as verification of the contents of the database. Under Recital 54, the maker has the burden to establish a substantial new investment.

laws of a Member State with its registered office, central administration, or principal place of business in the Community.[63] Nationals, habitual residents, and legal persons from third countries may only qualify on the basis of reciprocity.[64]

3.4. Remedies and Other Provisions

Member States are required to enact appropriate remedies for infringement including both copyright and unauthorized extraction or re-utilization of the contents of a database.[65]

In addition, legal provisions in the Member States relevant to the supply of database products and services continue to apply.[66] The Directive is also without prejudice to:
- Other Community measures such as data protection in Directive No. 95/46.[67]
- Application of Community or national competition rules.[68]
- Member State legislation on the broadcasting of audiovisual programs.[69]

4. Semiconductor Topographies

The topographies or lay-out designs of semiconductor products are specifically protected in the Community by Council Directive No. 87/54.[70] Here, too, the purpose is to establish harmonized standards in an important area of technology in order to promote innovation by safeguarding investments against misappropriation.[71]

4.1. Scope and Limitations

The Directive defines "topography" as a series of related images, however fixed or encoded:
- Representing the three-dimensional pattern of the layers of the semiconductor.

---

63 Articles 11(1) and (2) of Directive No. 96/9. Where only the registered office is located in the Community, company operations must be genuinely linked with the economy of a Member State on a continuing basis.

64 Article 11(3) and Recital 56 of Directive No. 96/9.

65 Article 12 and Recital 57 of Directive No. 96/9.

66 Article 13 and Recital 58 of Directive No. 96/9. The detailed recitation in Article 13 lists copyright and related rights, any other rights in the data, works, or material incorporated in a database, patent and design rights, trademarks, protection of national treasures, laws on restrictive practices and unfair competition, trade secrets, security, confidentiality, data protection and privacy, access to public documents, and the law of contract.

67 See Recital 48 of Directive No. 96/9 and Section 4 of Chapter 7 below. See also Article 3(2)(d) of the Commission proposal for utility models, at Section 1.3 and note 15 above, which excludes "presentations of information" from the category of inventions eligible for protection.

68 Recital 47 of Directive No. 96/9.

69 Recital 59 of Directive No. 96/9.

70 Council Directive No. 87/54 on the legal protection of topographies of semiconductor products, OJ No. L24/36 (January 27, 1987). Under Article 11(1), Member States were expected to enact appropriate implementing legislation by November 7, 1987. The Directive is consistent with Articles 31(c) and 35–38 of the WTO TRIPs agreement at note 3 above. The Community participated in prior negotiations on the Washington Treaty for protection of integrated circuits as intellectual property, but those arrangements were never ratified. See 23d EU General Report 1989 at ¶241 and 24th EU General Report 1990 at ¶147.

71 See Recitals 1–5 of Directive No. 87/54.

- With each image having all or part of the pattern of a surface of the semiconductor at any stage of its manufacture.[72]

Article 2(1) requires Member States to protect semiconductor topographies by exclusive rights in accordance with the Directive. To qualify, a topography must result from the creator's own intellectual effort and not be commonplace in the industry.[73] Protection covers the topography itself but not the concepts, processes, systems, techniques, or encoded information embodied in it.[74]

4.2. Protected Parties

The right applies in favor of the natural persons who create the topography if they are nationals or habitual residents of a Member State.[75] For items made in the course of employment or under contract, it may be given to the employer or person who commissioned the topography unless the terms stipulate otherwise.[76] Where no other eligible party exists, the right belongs to the qualified natural or legal person with exclusive authority throughout the Community who first commercially exploits a topography within a Member State which has not yet been exploited anywhere in the world.[77]

Under Article 3(5), protection extends to the successors in title of the rightholder. Articles 3(6) and (7) prescribe the mechanism for conferring exclusive rights on persons from third countries and in accordance with multilateral conventions.[78]

4.3. Registration Procedure

Article 4(1) enables Member States to specify that rights shall only arise or continue in existence if an application for registration is filed within two years of the first commercial exploitation. This includes the requirement to deposit material identifying or exemplifying the topography, as well as a statement on the date of initial exploitation where that precedes the application for registration.[79]

---

[72] Article 1(1)(b) of Directive No. 87/54. Article 1(1)(c) generally defines "commercial exploitation" as the sale, rental, leasing, or other method of distribution except under conditions of confidentiality such that no further distribution to third parties occurs. See also Articles 1(1)(a) and 1(2) which contain the definition of "semiconductor product" and provide for necessary adaptations in light of technical progress.

[73] Article 2(2) of Directive No. 87/54. Where a topography consists of elements which are commonplace, it is only protected to the extent that the combination of those elements taken as a whole satisfies the relevant criteria.

[74] Article 8 of Directive No. 87/54.

[75] Articles 3(1) and 3(3)(a) of Directive No. 87/54.

[76] Article 3(2) of Directive No. 87/54. In this situation, Article 3(3)(b) extends protection to nationals and habitual residents along with companies or other legal persons with a real and effective industrial or commercial establishment in a Member State.

[77] Article 3(4) of Directive No. 87/54.

[78] See, for example, Council Decision No. 94/824 on extension of the legal protection of semiconductor products to persons from a member of the WTO, OJ No. L349/201 (December 31, 1994).

[79] Article 4(2) preserves the confidentiality of trade secrets in the material deposited, but without prejudice to disclosure by order of competent authorities in any litigation concerning the validity or infringement of the exclusive rights.

The transfer of rights in topographies may also be subject to registration, but otherwise no additional formalities for obtaining or maintaining protection are permitted.[80] Under Article 4(6), legal remedies must be provided to rightholders who can establish that another party has applied for or obtained registration without authorization.

4.4. Restricted Acts and Exceptions

The exclusive rights granted by the Directive include authorizing or prohibiting:

- Reproduction of a protected topography.[81]
- Commercial exploitation or the related import of a topography or semiconductor manufactured from it.[82]

Under Article 5(2), Member States may nevertheless permit reproduction for private non-commercial use. In addition, Articles 5(3) and (4) make the exclusive rights inapplicable to reproduction for purposes of analyzing, evaluating, or teaching the concepts, processes, systems, or techniques embodied in the topography or the topography itself, as well as to any new design created from lawful evaluation of a protected item.

Finally, a person may not be prevented from commercially exploiting a semiconductor if he has no knowledge or reasonable grounds to believe that the product is protected at the time he acquires it.[83] However, the rightholder is entitled to adequate compensation for any such acts committed after the other person is on notice.

4.5. Term of Protection

Registered rights come into existence when the topography is first commercially exploited anywhere in the world or when the application for registration is filed, whichever is earlier.[84] Otherwise, Member States may elect the time of commercial exploitation or when the topography is initially fixed or encoded.[85]

For the period before rights exist by registration or commercial exploitation, there are legal remedies for protected parties who can establish that another person has fraudulently reproduced, commercially exploited, or imported a topography for that purpose.[86]

---

[80] Articles 4(3) and (5) of Directive No. 87/54. See also Article 6 which prohibits Member States from requiring compulsory licensing of the exclusive rights for the sole reason that a certain period of time has elapsed, automatically, and by operation of law.

[81] Article 5(1)(a) of Directive No. 87/54.

[82] Article 5(1)(b) of Directive No. 87/54. In accordance with the normal rule on exhaustion (see notes 28 and 48 above), the exclusive rights no longer apply after the topography or semiconductor has been put on the market in a Member State by the person entitled to authorize it or with his consent.

[83] Articles 5(6) and (7) of Directive No. 87/54.

[84] Article 7(1)(a) of Directive No. 87/54.

[85] Articles 7(1)(b) and (c) of Directive No. 87/54.

[86] Article 7(2) of Directive No. 87/54. This is without prejudice to other legal remedies to enforce the exclusive rights in accordance with the Directive.

The rights generally expire ten years after the first commercial exploitation or from the time the application for registration is filed if that is earlier.[87] For topographies which are not commercially exploited within 15 years from the initial fixation or encoding, any exclusive rights shall end and no others shall come into existence unless an application is filed within that period in those Member States which provide for registration.[88]

4.6. Other Provisions

Article 9 prescribes use of the "T" designation where Member State legislation permits an indication for semiconductor products manufactured from protected topographies.

Under Article 10, the Directive is without prejudice to:

- Legal provisions on patents and utility models.[89]
- Rights established by Member States in accordance with international agreements or copyright law restricting the reproduction of drawings or other artistic representations of topographies by copying them in two dimensions.
- Any protection under national law for topographies fixed or encoded before implementation of the Directive by the Member States.

[87] Article 7(3) of Directive No. 87/54.

[88] Article 7(4) of Directive No. 87/54.

[89] See also Article 8(1)(d) of Commission Regulation No. 240/96 on technology-transfer agreements at Section 3.5 of Chapter 5 above which defines "patents" to include semiconductor topographies.

CHAPTER 7

INTERNET AND ELECTRONIC COMMERCE

The dramatic growth of the Internet continues with profound implications for global communications and the international economy. Nevertheless, its widespread commercial use is a relatively recent development and a number of important regulatory issues remain unresolved. These are closely related to the general policies for the information society at Chapter 3, but include items in other key areas such as voice telephony, network governance and security, protection of personal data, and the emerging rules for electronic commerce. Each of these subjects is discussed in detail below.

1. Voice Telephony

As technology converges, it has become necessary to determine whether voice communications over the Internet should be considered telephony within the meaning of the comprehensive European telecommunications legislation in measures such as Commission Directive No. 90/388.[1] To date, the Commission has applied the following criteria in evaluating this question:[2]

- The communications must be the subject of a commercial offer.
- For the public.
- To and from public switched network termination points.
- Involving the direct transport and switching of speech in real-time.

In the Commission's judgment, voice transmission does not currently meet these requirements since it is only ancillary to an integrated package offered by Internet service providers which encompasses other elements such as browsing, e-mail, and the downloading of files and data. In addition, the quality of processing and transmission including voice mail is not yet equivalent to a standard real-time service.

For regulatory purposes, this means that Internet operators are not now subject to individual licensing procedures or the funding of universal service. Instead, the conditions are limited to a general authorization or declaration procedure which would normally be covered by their existing approvals for data-transmission or value-added services. The Commission intends to keep this situation under review and may revise their decision based on further technical and market developments.

---

1 See the citations in note 9 at Section 1 of Chapter 3 above as well as the discussion of technology convergence at Section 2 of Chapter 3.

2 Commission notice on the status of voice communications on the Internet under Community law and in particular pursuant to Directive No. 90/388, OJ No. C6/4 (January 10, 1998).

2. Internet Governance

This refers to management of the Internet including the domain names which enable computers to identify and communicate with each other on the network. The most widely-used generic top-level domains are the familiar ".com," ".net," and ".org."

Until October 1998, the system was operated by the Internet Assigned Names and Numbers Authority (IANA) in cooperation with Network Solutions Inc. (NSI), which acted as the registry for generic top-level domains and performed certain other functions under contract with the U.S. Government.[3] IANA has since been replaced by the Internet Corporation for Assigned Names and Numbers (ICANN), a private, non-profit entity headquartered in the U.S. (see *www.icann.org*). NSI retains a role in implementing a shared-registration system for the licensing of software and protocols to other parties who provide registry services for domain names.

The Community remains actively involved in Internet governance including the process which created ICANN as the successor to IANA.[4] Their emphasis throughout has been on basic principles to ensure proper management such as:

- Balanced international and private-sector participation.
- Effective competition in the allocation and administration of domain names.
- Conformity with agreed measures for the protection of intellectual property, personal data, and the resolution of disputes.
- Transparency and certainty for taxation and the prevention of fraud.

In addition, the Commission is considering the possible introduction of a new top-level domain "dot EU."[5] The purpose is to strengthen the identity and image of European companies and institutions on the Internet in order to accelerate the development of infrastructure and electronic commerce.

3. Network Security

In 1995 the Council highlighted the need for common security evaluation criteria as a prerequisite for trans-European applications in information technology products, services, and systems.[6] After a detailed analysis of network security, the Commission subsequently concluded that electronic services were being deterred by legitimate concerns about the confidentiality, integrity, and authenticity of data.[7] In particular, there were problems with

---

3 For a summary of the relevant background, see Commission press-release IP(99)596 (July 29, 1999).

4 See the Commission communication on international policy issues related to Internet governance, COM(98)111 (February 20, 1998), and the Commission press-releases IP(98)184 (February 25, 1998), IP(98)732 (July 29, 1998), IP(99)596 (July 29, 1999), and IP(00)355 (April 11, 2000).

5 See Commission press-release IP(00)95 (February 2, 2000) and Section 5.1 below.

6 Council Recommendation No. 95/144 on common information technology security evaluation criteria, OJ No. L93/27 (April 26, 1995). This was to be accompanied by harmonized criteria at the international level including mutual recognition of certificates.

7 Commission communication on ensuring trust and security in electronic communications – towards a European framework for digital signatures and encryption, COM(97)503 (October 8, 1997). See also Commission press-release IP(97)862 (October 8, 1997).

communications being used for illegal purposes, messages intercepted or manipulated, the validity of documents contested, and personal data improperly collected.

The sections that follow describe the efforts underway to address these issues through action to combat cybercrime, including harmful and illegal content, along with technical measures for electronic signatures, encryption, and conditional access. Legislation for the protection of personal data is covered at Section 4 below.

3.1. Cybercrime

Cybercrime encompasses various activities such as interference with electronic networks through hacking or piracy, their misuse for money laundering and other improper purposes, and content-related offenses as discussed in Section 3.2.

Proposed Community counter-measures include support for a Convention on Cybercrime within the Council of Europe which would improve international cooperation in the investigation and prosecution of illegal conduct involving computer systems and data.[8] This would supplement the substantive criminal law in areas such as child pornography, computer fraud and forgery, and crimes against the confidentiality and integrity of computer data.

In addition, the Commission is actively encouraging coordinated responses among the Member States and with appropriate third countries.[9] Forthcoming initiatives will seek to raise the awareness of service providers concerning the need for effective security against cybercrime including access to the latest encryption and other appropriate technologies.

3.2. Harmful and Illegal Content

This is an aspect of cybercrime where the regulatory aim is to strike an appropriate balance between free expression and other important values such as the protection of minors and human dignity.[10]

The most comprehensive treatment is in Council Recommendation No. 98/560 which applies to audiovisual and information services by whatever means including broadcasting, proprietary on-line systems, and the Internet.[11] The emphasis is on voluntary industry

---

[8] Common position adopted by the Council under Article 34 of the Treaty on European Union for negotiations relating to the Draft Convention on Cybercrime held in the Council of Europe, OJ No. L142/1 (June 5, 1999).

[9] Commission press-release IP(00)144 (February 10, 2000).

[10] For example, see the Council conclusions on the protection of minors in light of the development of digital audiovisual services, OJ No. C8/8 (January 12, 2000). Other provisions which relate to this subject include Article 1(2) of the common position on the Draft Cybercrime Convention at Section 3.1 and Recital 24 of Directive No. 98/84 on the legal protection of conditional access services at Section 3.4. See also the reference in note 8 at Section 1 of Chapter 3 to Directive No. 89/522 on television broadcast activities, OJ No. L298/23 (October 17, 1989), as amended by Directive No. 97/36, OJ No. L202/60 (July 30, 1997). Articles 22–22b of that legislation prescribe a range of measures for the protection of minors in order to ensure the free movement of television broadcasts.

[11] Council Recommendation No. 98/560 on development of the competitiveness of the European audiovisual and information services industry by promoting national frameworks aimed at achieving a comparable and

self-regulation through codes of conduct reflecting active participation by users, consumers, public authorities, parents, and educators. Any restrictions on privacy and freedom of expression must be necessary, non-discriminatory, and strictly proportional.

In exploring different solutions, the Recommendation notes that it may be helpful to distinguish between illegal content offensive to human dignity and content which is legal but nevertheless liable to harm minors by impairing their physical, mental, or moral development. It also recognizes that the global nature of communications may require a coordinated approach at the international level.

Recommendation No. 98/560 is reinforced by a multiannual Community action plan for promoting safe use of the Internet by combating illegal and harmful content.[12] This allocates funding of EUR 25 million for the period from January 1999 through December 2002.[13] Here, too, the focus is on industry self-regulation and content-monitoring programs in areas such as child pornography and material which incites hatred on grounds of race, sex, religion, nationality, or ethnic origin.[14] Detailed action lines are as follows:[15]

- Creating a safer environment through self-regulation, codes of conduct, and a European network of hot-lines.
- Developing filtering and rating systems along with appropriate multilateral agreements.
- Encouraging awareness so that parents, teachers, and children become more familiar with the potential drawbacks of the Internet and the means available to protect against undesirable content.
- Establishing support actions for assessing legal implications, coordinating with similar international initiatives, and evaluating the impact of Community measures.

3.3. Electronic Signatures

Electronic signatures enable the recipient of a message, with the help of a certification service provider, to verify the origin of data and determine whether it has been altered.[16]

The relevant provisions are in Directive No. 1999/93.[17] Under Article 1, the objective is to promote the use and legal recognition of electronic signatures and certification

---

effective level of protection of minors and human dignity, OJ No. L270/48 (October 7, 1998). The detailed Annex contains indicative guidelines for services provided to the public at a distance by electronic means. These do not cover radio or television broadcasting within the meaning of measures such as Directive No. 89/552 cited at note 10 above.

12 Decision No. 276/1999 of the European Parliament and Council adopting a multiannual Community action plan on promoting safer use of the Internet by combating illegal and harmful content on global networks, OJ No. L33/1 (February 6, 1999).

13 Articles 1(2) and (3) and Recital 11 of Decision No. 276/1999.

14 Article 3 of Decision No. 276/1999.

15 Annex I to Decision No. 276/1999.

16 See Commission press-releases IP(98)423 (May 13, 1998) and IP(99)915 (November 30, 1999).

17 Directive No. 1999/93 of the European Parliament and Council on a Community framework for electronic signatures, OJ No. L13/12 (January 19, 2000).

services.[18] Article 2 defines a number of key terms including:

- Electronic signature: data in electronic form which is associated with other electronic data and serves as a method of authentication.
- Advanced electronic signature: one which is uniquely capable of identifying the signatory, created using means maintained under the signatory's sole control, and which is linked to the data so that any subsequent alteration is detectable.
- Certificate: an electronic attestation which links signature verification data to a person and confirms their identity.
- Certification service provider: a natural person or entity which issues certificates and performs related services.
- Electronic signature product: hardware or software used by a provider for electronic signature services including their creation and verification.

Member States may not subject certification services to prior authorization, but it is permissible to establish voluntary accreditation programs to enhance professionalism.[19] In addition, each Member State is required to supervise certification service providers on their territory who issue qualified certificates to the public.[20] Under Article 3(5), the Commission may endorse standards for electronic signature products which create a presumption of compliance with applicable requirements. Services and products which comply with the Directive may be offered freely throughout the internal market.[21]

On the critical issue of legal recognition, Article 5(1) obliges Member States to ensure that advanced electronic signatures which are based on a qualified certificate and generated by a secure creation device:

- Satisfy the legal requirements of a signature for data in electronic form in the same manner as handwritten signatures for paper-based data.
- Are admissible as evidence in legal proceedings.[22]

The Directive contains rules on the liability of certification service providers[23] and for recognizing the validity of certificates issued by providers from third countries which meet prescribed criteria.[24] Under Article 8(1), service providers and national accreditation or supervisory bodies must comply with Directive No. 95/46 on the protection of personal

---

18 Article 13(1) calls on the Member States to enact appropriate implementing legislation by July 19, 2001. Recital 5 of the Directive makes clear that it is without prejudice to controls on exports of dual-use goods in accordance with Council Regulation No. 3381/94 and Council Decision No. 94/942 as discussed at Section 2 of Chapter 4 above.

19 Articles 3(1) and (2) of Directive No. 1999/93.

20 Article 3(3) of Directive No. 1999/93.

21 Articles 4(1) and (2) of Directive No. 1999/93.

22 This is reinforced by Article 5(2) which confirms that a signature may not be denied legal effect and admissibility solely on the grounds that it is in electronic form, not based on a qualified certificate or one issued by an accredited provider, or not generated by a secure signature creation device.

23 Articles 6(1)–(4) of Directive No. 1999/93. In accordance with Article 6(5), this is without prejudice to Council Directive No. 93/13 on unfair terms in consumer contracts cited in note 61 at Section 5.1 below.

24 Article 7 of Directive No. 1999/93.

data.[25] Finally, there are detailed standards for qualified certificates, service providers who issue them, and secure signature-creation devices and verification.[26]

3.4. Encryption and Conditional Access

Along with electronic signatures, encryption and conditional access services play a vital role in network security by preventing unauthorized interference. General policies in this area aim to stimulate the European industry for cryptographic products and services, develop interoperable standards and infrastructure, and dismantle unnecessary approval procedures for the export of dual-use encryption technology.[27]

In addition, specific legislation requires the Member States to provide legal protection for conditional access services.[28] The purpose is to safeguard lawful providers against illicit devices intended to circumvent technical security measures.[29]

Definitions in Article 2 of the Directive include:

- Protected service: television, radio, and information society services when provided for remuneration and based on conditional access, or the related provision of conditional access as a service in its own right.
- Conditional access: any technical measure or arrangement where access to the protected service in intelligible form is conditional on prior individual authorization.
- Conditional access device: equipment or software designed or adapted to give access to a protected service in intelligible form.
- Illicit device: equipment or software designed or adapted to give access without the authorization of the service provider.

Article 4 prohibits the manufacture, import, distribution, sale, rental, possession, installation, maintenance, or replacement of illicit devices for commercial purposes, as well as commercial communications to promote an illicit device.[30] There are sanctions for violations and injured parties are entitled to appropriate remedies including damages, injunctive relief, and the disposal of illicit devices outside normal commercial channels.[31]

The Directive is without prejudice to Community rules on competition and intellectual property, along with national laws which proscribe the private possession of illicit devices or for the protection of minors, public policy, or public security.[32]

---

[25] See the discussion at Section 4 below.

[26] Annexes I–IV of Directive No. 1999/93.

[27] See the citations at note 18 along with the discussion at Section 2 of Chapter 4 above.

[28] Directive No. 98/84 of the European Parliament and Council on the legal protection of services based on or consisting of conditional access, OJ No. L320/54 (November 28, 1998). Under Article 6(1), appropriate implementing measures are expected by May 28, 2000.

[29] Article 1 and Recitals 6 and 13 of Directive No. 98/84.

[30] Under Recital 14 of Directive No. 98/84, "commercial communication" covers all forms of advertising, direct marketing, sponsorship, sales promotion, and public relations.

[31] Articles 5(1) and (2) of Directive No. 98/84. Under Recital 22, national measures for sanctions and remedies may require the activities to be carried out with knowledge or reasonable grounds to know that the devices were illicit.

[32] Recitals 21 and 24 of Directive No. 98/84. See also Section 3.2 on harmful and illegal content.

4. Protection of Personal Data

As a corollary to the measures for network security, Directive No. 95/46 contains detailed rules concerning the privacy of individuals in the processing of personal data.[33] This is accompanied by similar legislation for the telecommunications sector.[34] The terms of Directive No. 95/46 are summarized below.

4.1. Scope and Limitations

The Directive covers the processing of personal data wholly or partly by automatic means, as well as non-automatic processing of items to be incorporated in a filing system.[35] There is an exclusion for operations involving public security, defense, and criminal matters, or which are performed by an individual in a purely private capacity.[36] It is generally without prejudice to the principle of public access to official documents and to the regulation of marketing activities aimed at consumers.[37]

Relevant definitions in Article 2 of the Directive include:

- Personal data: information relating to an identified or identifiable natural person (the "data subject").
- Identifiable person: one who can be identified, directly or indirectly, by reference to an identification number or one or more factors specific to his physical, physiological, mental, economic, cultural or social identity.[38]
- Processing: any operation or set of operations performed on personal data, whether or not by automatic means, such as collection, recording, organization, storage, adaptation or alteration, retrieval, consultation, use, disclosure, dissemination, alignment or combination, blocking, erasure, or destruction.[39]
- Controller: the natural or legal person, public authority, agency, or other body which alone or jointly determines the purposes and means of processing.
- Processor: a natural or legal person, public authority, agency, or other body which processes personal data on behalf of the controller.
- Data subject's consent: any freely given, specific, and informed indication which signifies agreement to the processing of personal data.

---

[33] Directive No. 95/46 of the European Parliament and Council on the protection of individuals with regard to the processing of personal data and on the free movement of such data, OJ No. L281/31 (November 23, 1995). With certain exceptions, Article 32 requires Member States to enact implementing legislation within three years.

[34] Directive No. 97/66 of the European Parliament and Council concerning the processing of personal data and the protection of privacy in the telecommunications sector, OJ No. L24/1 (January 30, 1998). In addition, there is a proposal for the equivalent protection of data within EU institutions since these are outside the scope of Directive No. 95/46. See Commission press-release IP(99)497 (July 15, 1999).

[35] Article 3(1) and Recital 27 of Directive No. 95/46. Recitals 14–16 indicate that, under appropriate circumstances, this may also include data in sound and images.

[36] Article 3(2) and Recitals 12 and 13 of Directive No. 95/46.

[37] Recitals 71 and 72 of Directive No. 95/46.

[38] See also Recital 26 of Directive No. 95/46.

[39] See also Recital 27 of Directive No. 95/46.

4.2. Applicable Law

Each Member State must apply the Directive to controllers established on their territory or other territories to which their national law extends.[40] Where equipment used for processing is located within a Member State, then it has jurisdiction even if the controller is established outside the Community unless the use is solely for purposes of transit.[41] The Directive is without prejudice to the rules of territoriality in criminal matters.[42]

4.3. Lawful Processing

Member States are required to determine the specific conditions for lawful processing in accordance with the rules prescribed by the Directive.[43] To protect the quality of personal data, Article 6[44] obliges the controller to ensure that it is:

- Processed fairly and lawfully.
- For specified, explicit, and legitimate purposes.
- Adequate, relevant, and not excessive in relation to those purposes.
- Accurate and up-to-date with reasonable steps taken to erase or correct data which is inaccurate or incomplete.
- In a form which does not permit identification of the data subject any longer than necessary.

In addition, processing is only lawful if done with the unambiguous consent of the data subject or where it is necessary in connection with a contract, the protection of his vital interests, compliance with a legal obligation of the controller, performance of tasks in the public interest or exercise of official authority, or in accordance with the legitimate interests of the controller or third parties unless overridden by the rights of the data subject.[45]

With certain exceptions, Member States must prohibit processing of data revealing racial or ethnic origin, political opinions, religious or philosophical beliefs, trade union membership, and health or sex life.[46] There are special rules for data relating to criminal offenses, security measures, administrative and civil cases, national identification numbers, and for journalistic, artistic, or literary purposes to the extent necessary to reconcile the right to privacy with freedom of expression.[47]

---

[40] Articles 4(1)(a) and (b), and Recitals 18 and 19 of Directive No. 95/46. When the same controller has affiliates established in several member States, each must comply with the relevant national obligations.

[41] Article 4(1)(c) and Recital 20 of Directive No. 95/46. Under these circumstances, Article 4(2) requires the controller to designate a representative established in the territory of the Member State regardless whether legal action may be initiated against the controller himself.

[42] Recital 21 of Directive No. 95/46.

[43] Article 5 and Recitals 22–27 of Directive No. 95/46.

[44] See also Recitals 28 and 29 of Directive No. 95/46. It is generally permissible for data to be processed or stored for historical, statistical, or scientific purposes as long as there are adequate safeguards.

[45] Article 7 and Recitals 30–32 of Directive No. 95/46.

[46] Articles 8(1)–(4) and Recitals 33–36 of Directive No. 95/46.

[47] Articles 8(5), 8(7), and 9 and Recitals 17 and 37 of Directive No. 95/46.

4.4. Rights of the Data Subject

When information is collected from the data subject, he must be advised of the identity of the controller or his representative, the purpose of the processing, and any other items necessary to ensure fairness such as the intended recipients, whether responses are voluntary, possible consequences of failure to reply, and rights of access and correction.[48] Similar rules apply where data is obtained from other sources.[49]

Under Article 12(a), the subject has the right to obtain the following from the controller at reasonable intervals and without excessive delay or expense:[50]

- Confirmation whether data relating to him is being processed along with the purposes, categories, and recipients.
- Communication of the data being processed and information as to its source.
- The logic for automatic processing in the case of any decisions in accordance with Article 15 as discussed immediately below.

Articles 12(b) and (c) enable the subject to correct, erase, or block data which is incomplete or inaccurate, and to require that recipients be notified unless that would be impossible or involve a disproportionate effort. Under appropriate circumstances, he may have the right to object to certain processing carried out for direct marketing or in the interest of the public, the controller, or third parties.[51] Finally, with specified exceptions, Article 15 entitles a person to be free of decisions which produce legal effects or significantly affect him based solely on automated data processing intended to evaluate personal characteristics such as performance at work, creditworthiness, reliability, and conduct.

4.5. Exemptions and Restrictions

Member States may restrict certain rights concerning the quality of data, information, and access[52] when necessary to safeguard:

- National or public security and defense.
- Measures relating to criminal enforcement or ethical requirements for regulated professions.
- Important economic or financial interests of the Member States or European Union including monetary, budgetary, and taxation matters.

---

48 Article 10 and Recital 38 of Directive No. 95/46. These requirements do not apply if the subject already has the relevant information.

49 Article 11(1) and Recital 39 of Directive No. 95/46. The information must be provided at the time the data is recorded or, if disclosure to a third party is contemplated, no later than when that occurs. Subject to appropriate safeguards, Article 11(2) and Recital 40 permit exceptions where this would be impossible or involve disproportionate effort as in processing for statistical, historical, or scientific purposes.

50 See also Recitals 41 and 42 of Directive No. 95/46 which authorize certain exceptions to the subject's right of access in specified cases such as medical data, trade secrets, or intellectual property including computer software.

51 Article 14 and Recital 45 of Directive No. 95/46.

52 Article 13(1) and Recitals 43 and 44 of Directive No. 95/46. Under Article 13(2), certain restrictions are also permitted for data processed solely for scientific or statistical purposes.

- Certain monitoring, inspection, or regulatory functions in connection with the exercise of official authority.
- Protection of the data subject or the rights and freedom of others.

4.6. Remedies and Sanctions

In addition to administrative procedures, Member States must establish judicial remedies and effective sanctions for breach of the rights prescribed by national law in accordance with the Directive.[53] The controller is liable for compensation to any person injured by an unlawful processing operation or other violation of the relevant provisions unless he can prove that he is not responsible for the event causing the damage.[54]

4.7. Transfer to Third Countries

To prevent circumvention, Article 25(1) only permits personal data to be transferred to third countries which ensure an adequate level of protection. Under Article 25(2), this is evaluated in light of all the circumstances including the nature of the data, purpose and duration of processing, countries of origin and final destination, and the law, professional rules, and security measures which apply in the third country. Other terms cover procedures for implementation, negotiations to remedy deficiencies, and exceptions which may authorize transfers under specified conditions even when adequate protection does not exist.[55]

These requirements resulted in a protracted dispute with the U.S. which was tentatively resolved in March 2000.[56] The central issue was how to reconcile the Community's legislative approach to protection with the self-regulatory system in the U.S. Under the proposed solution for a "safe harbor" arrangement, the U.S. Department of Commerce will establish a list of companies which agree to abide by certain rules and enforcement provisions. Compliance will be monitored by the private sector but with sanctions in accordance with U.S. legislation which prohibits misrepresentation and deceptive trade practices. Before formal approval, the Commission must obtain the support of Member States and the European Parliament.

4.8. Other Provisions

Finally, the Directive contains the following additional provisions to help ensure that it is implemented properly:

- Measures for confidentiality and security of processing which are applicable to the controller, processor, and their representatives.[57]

---

[53] Articles 22 and 24 and Recital 55 of Directive No. 95/46.

[54] Article 23 and Recital 55 of Directive No. 95/46.

[55] Articles 25(3)–(6) and 26 and Recitals 56–60 of Directive No. 95/46.

[56] See Commission press-release IP(00)301 (March 29, 2000).

[57] Articles 16 and 17 and Recitals 46 and 47 of Directive No. 95/46.

- Codes of conduct to reinforce the national legislation adopted in accordance with the Directive.[58]
- Establishment of supervisory authorities within the Member States, and a working party and committee at Community level, to perform monitoring, administrative, and advisory functions.[59]

5. Electronic Commerce

5.1. General

Along with the rules on product liability considered earlier,[60] other measures at European level deal generally with areas such as advertising, consumer protection, and financial services.[61] Typically, however, these were not drafted with specific reference to the information society or with the particular requirements of electronic commerce in mind.

European authorities are now beginning to address this situation in accordance with the basic approach[62] outlined below:

- Application of traditional principles to on-line services, but with the recognition that it may be necessary to clarify and adapt the existing legal framework and enforcement mechanisms.
- Regulatory efforts to be flexible and not overly restrictive in order to accommodate the dynamic characteristics of the new technology.
- Active consultation and participation of the private sector with reliance on industry self-regulation and codes of conduct to the extent possible.
- Negotiation of appropriate arrangements for voluntary multilateral cooperation to remove obstacles to electronic commerce at the international level.[63]

---

[58] Article 27 and Recital 61 of Directive No. 95/46.

[59] Articles 18–21 and 28–31 and Recitals 48–54 and 62–67 of Directive No. 95/46.

[60] See the discussion at Section 5 of Chapter 3 above.

[61] For example, see Directive No. 1999/44 of the European Parliament and Council on certain aspects of the sale of consumer goods and associated guarantees, OJ No. L171/12 (July 7, 1999); Directive No. 98/27 of the European Parliament and Council on injunctions for the protection of consumer interests, OJ No. L166/51 (June 11, 1998); Commission Recommendation No. 98/257 on the principles applicable to bodies responsible for out-of-court settlement of consumer disputes, OJ No. L115/31 (April 17, 1998); Directive No. 97/55 of the European Parliament and Council on comparative advertising, OJ No. L290/18 (October 23, 1997); Directive No. 97/9 of the European Parliament and Council on investor compensation schemes, OJ No. L84/22 (March 26, 1997); Directive No. 97/5 of the European Parliament and Council on cross-border credit transfers, OJ No. L43/25 (February 14, 1997); Council Directive No. 93/22 on investment services in the securities field, OJ No. L141/27 (June 11, 1993); Council Directive No. 93/13 on unfair terms in consumer contracts, OJ No. L95/29 (April 21, 1993); and Council Directive No. 84/450 on misleading advertising, OJ No. L250/17 (September 19, 1984).

[62] See the Commission communication on a European initiative for electronic commerce, COM(97)157 (April 15, 1997), and the Commission press-releases IP(98)114 (February 4, 1998), IP(98)196 (February 26, 1998), and IP(98)586 (June 30, 1998).

[63] For example, see Commission press-release IP(99)966 (December 9, 1999) which endorses OECD guidelines for consumer protection in electronic commerce based on the principle that safeguards should be equivalent to those available for off-line transactions.

At a special meeting in Lisbon on March 23 and 24, 2000, the European Council adopted a comprehensive "e-Europe" initiative intended to reinforce this with specific actions to accelerate the development of electronic commerce, lower the cost of Internet access, and remedy the "skills gap" for information technology in the Community.[64] These include an "e-Europe" website to consolidate information on progress in this area,[65] a proposal for a new Internet top-level domain "dot EU,"[66] an "e-learning" program for education and training,[67] and an "e-confidence" forum for exchanges in the field of alternative dispute resolution.[68] See also Section 3.3 of Chapter 2 and Section 1 of Chapter 3 above.

The remaining sections cover the Directive for electronic commerce, along with other important measures for distance selling, electronic data interchange, electronic payment, and taxation.

5.2. E-Commerce Directive

The centerpiece of current legislation is the Directive for a coherent and integrated approach to the legal aspects of electronic commerce in the Community.[69] Under Articles 1(1) and (2), the purpose is to ensure the free movement of information society services by harmonizing the laws of the Member States in key areas. The Directive does not apply to taxation, protection of personal data, matters subject to cartel law, certain forms of gambling, activities of notaries, or representation of clients in judicial proceedings.[70] It is without prejudice to measures for public health, consumer welfare, and the promotion of cultural and linguistic diversity.[71]

Definitions in Article 2 include:

- Information society services: services within the meaning of Directives No. 98/34, as amended, and No. 98/84.[72] The intention is to cover any service normally provided for

---

64 See the Commission press-releases IP(99)953 (December 8, 1999) and IP(00)239 (March 9, 2000), and the Presidency conclusions in Lisbon at Doc. PRES(00)900 (March 28, 2000). For background, see the Commission communication: e-Europe – an information society for all, COM(99)687 (December 8, 1999).

65 Commission press-release IP(00)320 (March 31, 2000).

66 Commission press-release IP(00)95 (February 2, 2000) and Section 2 above.

67 Commission press-releases IP(00)234 (March 9, 2000) and IP(00)522 (May 24, 2000).

68 Commission press-release IP(00)312 (March 30, 2000). Alternative dispute resolution is viewed as particularly useful in providing a low-cost, rapid, and effective method for dealing with potential problems in cross-border transactions and electronic commerce. Other Community support involves co-financing of the Web-Trader program for on-line certification and remedies, and promotion of a European Extra-Judicial Network for clearinghouses in each Member State to furnish consumers with information on procedures for dispute settlement in the country where the supplier is located. See Commission press-releases IP(00)445 (May 5, 2000), IP(00)312 (March 30, 2000), and IP(00)274 (March 20, 2000).

69 The latest published version is Common Position No. 22/2000 for a Directive of the European Parliament and Council on certain legal aspects of information society services, in particular electronic commerce, in the internal market, OJ No. C128/32 (May 8, 2000). According to the Commission, this was finally enacted without further amendment. See Commission press-release IP(00)442 (May 4, 2000). Article 22(1) requires Member States to implement the Directive within 18 months after entry into force.

70 Article 1(5) and Recitals 12–16.

71 Articles 1(3) and (6) and Recitals 10 and 11, and 63 and 64. This includes legislation for consumer protection such as the items cited at Section 5.1 as well as Directive No. 97/7 on distance selling at Section 5.3 below.

72 Directives No. 98/34, as amended, and No. 98/84 are discussed at Section 5.2 of Chapter 2 and Section 3.4 of this chapter, respectively.

remuneration, at a distance, by means of electronic equipment for the processing and storage of data, and at the individual request of a recipient.[73]

- Established service provider: one who effectively pursues an economic activity using a fixed establishment for an indefinite period. The presence and use of technical means to provide the service do not constitute such an establishment.[74]
- Commercial communication: any form designed to promote goods, services, or the image of someone pursuing a commercial or industrial activity, craft, or liberal profession. This does not include information about direct access to the activity such as domain names or e-mail addresses, or communications compiled independently without financial consideration.

Articles 3(1) and (2) require service providers to comply with the Directive in the Member State where they are established, and generally prohibit other Member States from interfering with the freedom to provide those services.[75] However, this does not extend to the fields listed in the Annex which include certain intellectual property measures such as Directives No. 96/9 and No. 87/54 on the legal protection of databases and semiconductor topographies, respectively.[76] In addition, certain derogations are permitted for reasons of consumer protection and public health, policy, and security.[77] The Directive does not apply to providers established in third countries although Community rules should be consistent with international norms in view of the global nature of electronic commerce.[78]

Activities of providers do not require prior authorization except in accordance with general measures which are not exclusively targeted at information society services.[79] Recipients must be given essential information about the service provider in a direct, permanent, and easily accessible manner including clear and unambiguous data on price.[80] Other conditions apply to commercial communications, unsolicited messages, and the regulated professions.[81]

Subject to certain limitations, Article 9(1) enables contracts to be made electronically and prohibits legal requirements which impair their validity and effective use.[82]

---

73 Recital 17 of the Directive. Under Recital 18, this also includes services which are not remunerated such as those offering on-line information, commercial communications, or tools for search, access, and retrieval of data. These are presumably funded by advertising or other forms of sponsorship.

74 For services provided over an Internet website, Recital 19 confirms that the place of establishment is not where the site is accessible or where supporting technology is located.

75 See also Recitals 22 and 57 concerning the place of establishment. For suppliers established in more than one territory, Recital 19 indicates that jurisdiction is where the center of activity is located.

76 Article 3(3) of the Directive. For details on Directives No. 96/9 and No. 87/54, see Sections 3 and 4 of Chapter 6 above.

77 Article 3(4) and Recitals 24–27.

78 Recitals 58–62 of the Directive.

79 Articles 4(1) and (2) of the Directive.

80 Articles 5(1) and (2) of the Directive.

81 Articles 6–8 and Recitals 29–33.

82 Article 9(2) permits exceptions for certain contracts concerning real estate, suretyship, family law, succession, or which involve courts or public authorities. See also Recitals 34–38.

Prior to an order being placed, Article 10 generally entitles the recipient to be advised of the technical steps for concluding the contract and identifying errors in a clear, comprehensible, and unambiguous manner.[83] Under Article 11, service providers must acknowledge receipt of an order without undue delay including advance information to the recipient on appropriate, effective, and accessible means for correcting any errors.

Special provisions cover the liability of intermediaries when hosting, monitoring, acting as a conduit, or performing caching services for the automatic and temporary storage of information.[84] Finally, procedures for implementation include codes of conduct, out-of-court dispute settlement, judicial actions, cooperation between national authorities, electronic media, and sanctions which must be effective, proportionate, and dissuasive.[85]

5.3. Distance Selling

In addition to the E-Commerce Directive, another important measure is Directive No. 97/7 on the protection of consumers in distance contracts.[86]

Article 2(1) defines "distance contract" as an agreement for goods or services in accordance with an organized program where the supplier makes exclusive use of distance communications up to the point the contract is formed. Distance communications include regular and e-mail, telephone, fax, radio, videophone and videotext, teleshopping, catalogue, and press advertising with order form.[87]

Before concluding any distance contract, the consumer must be advised of the identity of the supplier, main characteristics and price of the goods or services, arrangements for payment and delivery, right of withdrawal, period for which the offer or price remains valid, and minimum duration of the contract in cases of recurring performance.[88] Article 5 ensures timely confirmation of the relevant details in writing or another durable medium. The consumer has at least seven working days to withdraw without penalty and without giving any reason.[89] In addition, Member States may place the burden of proof on the supplier to establish compliance with the applicable requirements.[90]

The Directive does not apply to contracts for financial services such as banking, investments, dealings in futures or options, and insurance or reinsurance operations.[91] To remedy that deficiency, the Commission has proposed a specific Directive on the distance

---

83 See also Recital 37 of the Directive.

84 Articles 12–15 and Recitals 40–48 and 50.

85 Articles 16–20 and Recitals 49 and 51–54.

86 Directive No. 97/7 of the European Parliament and Council on the protection of consumers in respect of distance contracts, OJ No. L144/19 (June 14, 1997). Article 15 requires Member States to implement the Directive within three years.

87 Article 2(4) and Annex I of Directive No. 97/7.

88 Article 4(1) of Directive No. 97/7.

89 Article 6(1) of Directive No. 97/7. The only charge that may be imposed is the direct cost of returning the goods. Under Article 6(3), there are certain exceptions to the right of withdrawal including contracts involving the supply of audio or video recordings or computer software where the items were unsealed by the consumer.

90 Article 11(3) of Directive No. 97/7.

91 Article 3(1) and Annex II of Directive No. 97/7.

marketing of consumer financial services which would complement the provisions in Directive No. 97/7.[92]

5.4. Electronic Data Interchange

As part of the program for electronic data interchange (EDI) at Section 4 of Chapter 3 above, the Commission endorsed a European Model Agreement for the exchange of electronic messages between parties.[93] This defines EDI as the electronic transfer of commercial and administrative data from one computer to another using an agreed standard to structure a message.[94] An EDI message is a set of segments based on the agreed standard, prepared in computer-readable format, and capable of being processed automatically and unambiguously.[95]

A contract comes into existence when the EDI message constituting acceptance reaches the computer system of the party making the offer.[96] To the extent permitted by national law, the records of EDI messages maintained in accordance with the Agreement shall be admissible in court and serve as prima facie evidence of the relevant facts.[97] Other elements of the Model Agreement include processing, security, and confidentiality of EDI messages, operational requirements, technical specifications, liability, dispute resolution, and applicable law.

5.5. Electronic Payment

To promote consumer confidence and retail acceptance in this area, there was a recommendation from the Commission to the Member States in 1997 concerning transactions by electronic payment and the relationship between issuer and holder.[98] Under Article 1(1), this relates to the electronic transfer of funds as well as cash withdrawals including the loading and unloading of electronic money at automated teller machines. The definitions in Article 2 cover both remote access payment and electronic money instruments such as stored-value cards. There are provisions on the terms and conditions for issuance and use of electronic payment instruments, along with information subsequent to a transaction, obligations and liability of the issuer and holder, and procedures for notification and settlement of disputes. Member States were invited to take necessary measures by December 1998.

---

92 Proposal for a Directive of the European Parliament and Council concerning the distance marketing of consumer financial services and amending Council Directive No. 90/619 and Directives No. 97/7 and No. 98/27, OJ No. C385/10 (December 11, 1998). See also Commission press-releases IP(98)891 (October 14, 1998) and IP(99)559 (July 26, 1999).

93 Commission Recommendation No. 94/820 on the legal aspects of electronic data interchange, OJ No. L338/98 (December 28, 1994). The text of the EDI Model Agreement is at Annex I of the Commission Recommendation.

94 Article 2.2 of the EDI Model Agreement.

95 Article 2.3 of the EDI Model Agreement.

96 Article 3.3 of the EDI Model Agreement.

97 Article 4 of the EDI Model Agreement.

98 Commission Recommendation No. 97/489 concerning transactions by electronic payment instruments and in particular the relationship between issuer and holder, OJ No. L208/52 (August 2, 1997).

In addition, two proposed Directives would apply specifically to the issuance of electronic money.[99] The first would amend the definition of "credit institution" in existing banking legislation to cover this activity.[100] The second would introduce a separate system of prudential supervision for electronic monetary institutions which is less cumbersome than the rules for credit institutions generally.[101] To qualify, these entities would have to restrict their business to the issuance of electronic money and other ancillary functions which would not enable them to grant any form of credit.[102]

5.6. Taxation

This subject is critical to the development of electronic commerce, but many important details remain unresolved. Nevertheless, discussions continue within international forums such as the OECD in an effort to achieve consensus based on established principles of neutrality and non-discrimination. The Community has taken the lead on issues of indirect or value-added taxation (VAT) in accordance with the following guidelines:[103]

- The existing system should be adapted but without any new taxes specifically aimed at electronic commerce.
- For VAT purposes, the supply of products over electronic networks should be considered a "service" rather than a "good."
- To promote neutrality, services supplied for consumption within the Community should be taxed there. Those provided within the Community for consumption elsewhere should not be taxed and input VAT should be deductible.
- For ease of administration, systems should be compatible with commercial practice and compliance as simple as possible consistent with preventing abuse. Taxpayers should be able to account for and submit VAT declarations electronically.

---

[99] The latest published versions are in Common Position No. 8/2000 on the taking-up, pursuit, and prudential supervision of the business of electronic money institutions, OJ No. C26/1 (January 28, 2000), and Common Position No. 9/2000 amending Directive No. 77/780 on the taking-up and pursuit of the business of credit institutions, OJ No. C26/12 (January 28, 2000). See also Commission press-release IP(98)727 (July 29, 1998).

[100] Article 1(4) of Common Position No. 8/2000 and Article 1(1)(b) and Recitals 2 and 3 of Common Position No. 9/2000.

[101] Article 1(1) and Recitals 7 and 10 of Common Position No. 8/2000.

[102] Article 1(5) of Common Position No. 8/2000.

[103] Commission press-release IP(98)535 (June 17, 1998).

INDEX